How to Use This Book

Look for these special features in this book:

SIDEBARS, **CHARTS**, **GRAPHS**, and original **MAPS** expand your understanding of what's being discussed—and also make useful sources for classroom reports.

FAQs answer common **F**requently **A**sked **Q**uestions about people, places, and things.

WOW FACTORS offer "Who knew?" facts to keep you thinking.

WITHDRAWN

TRAVEL GUIDE gives you tips on exploring the state—either in person or right from your chair!

PROJECT ROOM provides fun ideas for school assignments and incredible research projects. Plus, there's a guide to primary sources—what they are and how to cite them.

Please note: All statistics are as up-to-date as possible at the time of publication.

Consultants: Thomas H. Appleton Jr., Professor of History, Eastern Kentucky University; William Loren Katz; Anna E. Watson, Kentucky Geological Survey

Book production by The Design Lab

Library of Congress Cataloging-in-Publication Data
Santella, Andrew.
 Kentucky / by Andrew Santella.
    p. cm.—(America the beautiful)
 Includes bibliographical references and index.
 ISBN-13: 978-0-531-18574-2
 ISBN-10: 0-531-18574-5
 1. Kentucky—Juvenile literature. 2. Kentucky—History—Juvenile
literature. I. Title. II. Series.
 F451.3.S26 2008
 976.9—dc22   2007004803

1 2 3 4 5 6 7 8 9 10 R 17 16 15 14 13 12 11 10 09 08

AMERICA ★ THE ★ BEAUTIFUL

Kentucky

BY ANDREW SANTELLA

Third Series

Children's Press®
An Imprint of Scholastic Inc.
New York ★ Toronto ★ London ★ Auckland ★ Sydney
Mexico City ★ New Delhi ★ Hong Kong
Danbury, Connecticut

CONTENTS

4 GROWTH AND CHANGE

A young and growing state produces national leaders—and is torn by Civil War. . . . **44**

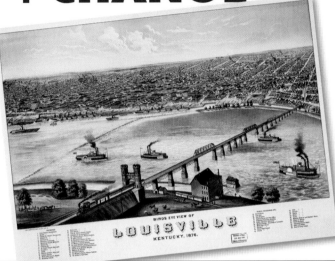

BIRDS EYE VIEW OF LOUISVILLE KENTUCKY, 1876.

MORE MODERN TIMES

5

Big coal mines bring big changes to Kentucky. And African Americans and others struggle for civil rights. **56**

PROJECT ROOM

★

9 TRAVEL GUIDE

Explore the back roads. Enjoy the city streets. History, horses, music, and more: it's all in Kentucky. **104**

N
W E
S

0   50
Miles

INDIANA

OHIO

The Knobs

COVINGTON

Kentucky Derby at
Churchill Downs

Ohio

FRANKFORT

Fort Knox

Fort Boonesborough
State Park

ILLINOIS

Ohio River

Ohio

LOUISVILLE

LEXINGTON

Kentucky

Black
Mountain

OWENSBORO

KENTUCKY

Berea
College

Mountains

Mammoth
Cave

Mississippi

BOWLING GREEN

Fisher-Ridge
Cave

Cumberland

Appalachian

VIRGINIA

MISSOURI

Kentucky
Lake

Appalachian
Mountains

Mississippi River

Trail of Tears
Commemorative
Park

Tallest
Tree in
Kentucky

Cumberland Gap
National
Historic Park

CUMBERLAND
GAP

NORTH
CAROLINA

MISSISSIPPI

ALABAMA

TENNESSEE

GEORGIA

PENNSYLVANIA

NEW JERSEY

WEST VIRGINIA

SOUTH CAROLINA

ATLANTIC OCEAN

KENTUCKY

Welcome to Kentucky!

HOW DID KENTUCKY GET ITS NAME?

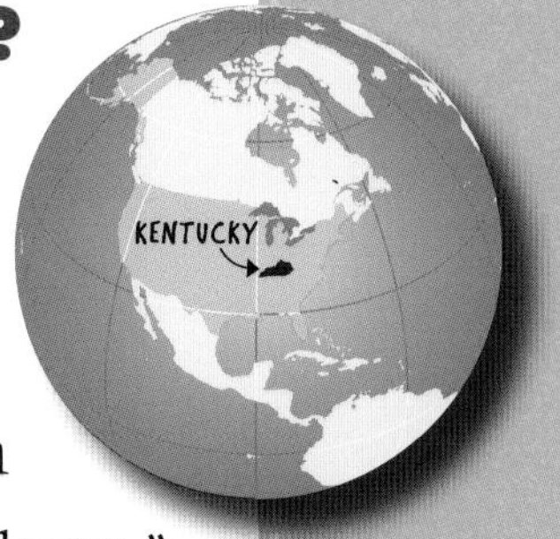

No one knows for sure where the name *Kentucky* comes from. Some people say that it comes from a Wyandot word meaning "land of tomorrow." Others say it comes from an Iroquoian word meaning "place of meadows." In the 1700s, European settlers along the eastern edge of the Appalachian Mountains heard tales of a rich land beyond the mountains. They called it Kentucke or Cantucky. No matter what they called it, just about everyone who visited agreed on one thing: this land of rivers, forests, and meadows was the place to be. An early land surveyor summed it up after he visited Kentucky in 1775: "A richer and more beautiful country than this, I believe has never been seen in America yet."

8

READ ABOUT

A river flows over
a rocky waterfall
in Cumberland
Falls State Resort.

CHAPTER ONE

LAND

★

"**A** SERIES OF WONDERS." That's how pioneer Daniel Boone described Kentucky's natural world after his first extended visit in 1769. Across the state, miles of scenic rivers run through steep gorges and meander across wide valleys. The state's lowest point rests along the Mississippi River, at 257 feet (78 meters). Rugged mountains with dense forests cover much of Kentucky's eastern region, including the state's highest point—Black Mountain at 4,145 feet (1,263 m). From plunging waterfalls to deep, mysterious caves, Kentucky packs a lot of amazing sights into its 40,409 square miles (104,659 square kilometers).

Kentucky is home to two of the world's longest caves. Besides Mammoth Cave, the Fisher-Ridge cave system ranks sixth in the world at 85 miles (137 km) long.

ANCIENT BEGINNINGS

From more than 500 million to almost 300 million years ago, shallow seas covered Kentucky. When the sea's creatures died, their shells and bones sank to the seafloor. Over millions of years, these shells mixed with sand and mud and hardened to form limestone. When the sea receded, that limestone was left exposed at the earth's surface. Over many years, rainwater seeped down through cracks in the soft rock. Underground streams and rivers formed and etched paths through the limestone beds. Some of those passages grew larger and larger, until they eventually became caves with fabulous crystal formations and unique animal life. Mammoth Cave, near what is now Bowling Green, is the longest cave system in the world!

Starting approximately 320 million years ago, lush, heavily forested swamps covered much of what is now Kentucky. Dead and decaying plants and trees fell and sank to the bottom of swamps, transforming into layer upon layer of a soggy material called peat. Over many thousands of years, as the climate and the earth's surface changed, great rivers left deposits of clay and sand on top of the peat. Under the great weight of the deep layers of material, the peat slowly changed into coal. Today, mining that coal is one of Kentucky's key industries.

About 300 million years ago, collisions between the plates that make up the earth's surface began to change the face of the eastern United States. Over many years, these collisions forced some landmasses upward, including those that contained the ancient seabeds and swamps of Kentucky. These upheavals eventually formed the Appalachian Mountains, which run through eastern Kentucky.

Kentucky Topography

Use the color-coded elevation chart to see on the map Kentucky's high points (dark red to orange) and low points (green to dark green). Elevation is measured as the distance above or below sea level.

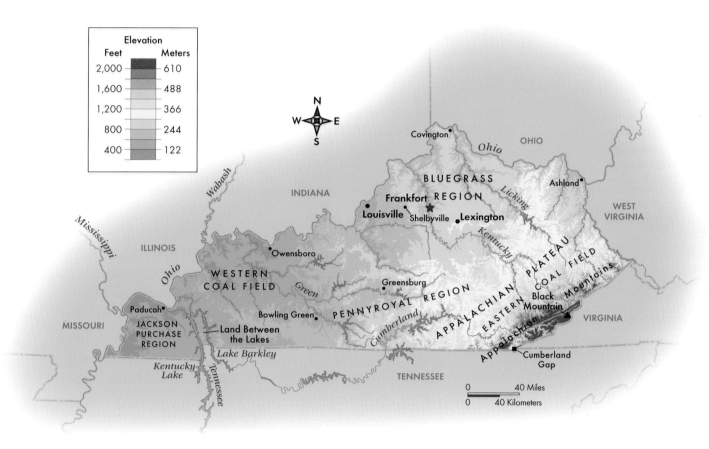

LAND REGIONS

Two great rivers help form Kentucky's boundaries: the Ohio to the north, and the Mississippi to the west. The rough and beautiful Appalachian Mountains stand along its eastern border. Kentucky has five major land regions: the Eastern Kentucky Coal Field, the Bluegrass, the Pennyroyal, the Western Kentucky Coal Field, and the Jackson Purchase.

Kentucky Geo-Facts

Along with the state's geographical highlights, this chart ranks Kentucky's land, water, and total area compared to all other states.

Total area; rank	40,409 square miles (104,659 sq km); 37th
Land; rank	39,728 square miles (102,896 sq km); 36th
Water; rank	681 square miles (1,764 sq km); 38th
Inland water; rank	681 square miles (1,764 sq km); 31st
Geographic center	Marion, 3 miles (5 km) north-northwest of Lebanon
Latitude	36° 30′ N to 39° 9′ N
Longitude	81° 58′ W to 89° 34′ W
Highest point	Black Mountain at 4,145 feet (1,263 m)
Lowest point	At the Mississippi River, 257 feet (78 m)
Largest city	Louisville
Longest river	Ohio River

Source: U.S. Census Bureau

As the 36th-largest state, Kentucky is roughly the size of Iceland and about half the size of Minnesota.

WORD TO KNOW

tributaries *smaller rivers that flow into a larger river*

The Eastern Kentucky Coal Field

Kentucky is a major producer of coal in the country, and most of the state's coal comes from the Eastern Kentucky Coal Field. The Appalachian Mountains dominate the heavily forested coalfield, which is also home to some of the state's most impressive scenery. The Cumberland and Kentucky rivers and their **tributaries** cut through this region. In many places, the rivers tumble over scenic waterfalls. In other places, running water has carved natural bridges and other stunning formations out of rock. High cliffs and deep gorges dot the landscape. The historic Cumberland Gap is in the southeasternmost corner of the state. Kentucky's highest point, Black Mountain (4,145 feet, or 1,263 m), also lies inside the Eastern Kentucky Coal Field.

The Bluegrass

The Bluegrass region of north-central Kentucky is home to some of the state's richest farmland. The Inner Bluegrass is an area of fertile, rolling landscapes and is famed for its horse farms. With white fences stretching into the distance and horses grazing on lush pastures, these farms have become a symbol of Kentucky's beauty. A 230-mile (370 km) range of steep, cone-shaped hills sets the Bluegrass off from neighboring

A horse farm in Lexington, which lies in the Inner Bluegrass region

regions. **Sandstone** or limestone caps many of these hills, called The Knobs. Over thousands of years, wind and water have **eroded** their slopes to create distinctive shapes.

The Bluegrass is home to some of Kentucky's biggest cities. The Ohio River city of Louisville is in the Outer Bluegrass, at the western edge of the region. Covington and the other cities of the Northern Kentucky Metropolitan Area are at the northern edge of the Outer Bluegrass. Lexington, home of the University of Kentucky, lies in the Inner Bluegrass, as does the state's capital, Frankfort.

WORDS TO KNOW

sandstone *a type of rock made of sand cemented together by another material*

eroded *slowly eaten away at and destroyed*

STEPHEN BISHOP: UNDERGROUND EXPLORER

The Pennyroyal's Mammoth Cave became a popular tourist site in the 1800s. One of its first and most famous tour guides was an enslaved man named Stephen Bishop (1821–1857). He explored more deeply into the cave than anyone else before him. He stretched a ladder across the cave's famous Bottomless Pit and crawled across. He also discovered artifacts—signs that Native Americans had explored the cave much earlier.

Want to know more? See www.nps.gov/maca/stephen.pdf

Mammoth Cave is part of a system of connected limestone caverns found in the Pennyroyal region.

The Pennyroyal

An underground world of dark chambers and narrow passages with names such as Corkscrew Way and Agony Avenue lies beneath the Pennyroyal (also known as the Pennyrile). Kentucky's largest land region, the Pennyroyal spreads along much of the state's southern border with Tennessee and extends north in places to the Ohio River. It is named for a kind of mint that grows throughout the region. High cliffs, or **escarpments**, mark its boundaries. In the western end of the region, you'll find a popular recreation area called the Land Between the Lakes. It lies between two human-made lakes— Kentucky Lake and Lake Barkley— formed by dams on the Cumberland and Tennessee rivers.

The Western Kentucky Coal Field

An almost circular region just south of the Ohio River, the Western Kentucky Coal Field is part of the U.S. Interior Coal Field, which extends into Indiana and Illinois. The area's coal mines produce about one-quarter of Kentucky's coal. Sometimes called the Shawnee Hills region, it is also one of the state's prime farming areas. Farms here produce corn, soybeans, wheat, and other crops, and raise hogs and beef cattle.

The Jackson Purchase

The Jackson Purchase got its name because it was part of a tract purchased by General Andrew Jackson (later president of the United States) from the Chickasaw people in 1818. The smallest of Kentucky's regions, the Jackson Purchase covers just eight counties and 2,400 square miles (6,200 sq km). Fertile soil that makes for good farming covers much of the area. In other places, wetlands provide habitats for many species of wildlife. Inhabitants who lived in the area about 1,000 years ago left behind the Wickliffe Mounds, part of an ancient village at the junction of the Ohio and Mississippi rivers.

MINI-BIO

JOHN FILSON: KENTUCKY'S FIRST AUTHOR

John Filson (c. 1753–1788) was the writer who helped make Kentucky famous. A teacher, author, and adventurer, Filson was born in Pennsylvania but moved to Lexington, Kentucky, in 1783. There he began to interview Kentuckians about their natural environment. In 1784, he published The Discovery, Settlement and Present State of Kentucke, a book that described the "beautiful landscape" of Kentucky so well that it helped attract new settlers to the area. Filson also told of the exploits of Daniel Boone, making the pioneer famous around the world.

? Want to know more? See www. famousamericans.net/johnfilson/

WORD TO KNOW

escarpments *long, steep cliffs*

Weather Report

This chart shows record temperatures (high and low) for the state, as well as average temperatures (July and January) and average annual precipitation.

Record high temperature . . . . 114°F (46°C)
    at Greensburg on July 28, 1930
Record low temperature . . . . –37°F (–38°C)
    at Shelbyville on January 19, 1994
Average July temperature . . . . 78°F (26°C)
Average January temperature . . . . 33°F (1°C)
Average annual precipitation . . . . 45 inches (114 cm)

Source: National Climatic Data Center, NESDIS, NOAA, U.S. Department of Commerce

CLIMATE

Kentucky's climate is moderate, which means it usually isn't extremely hot or extremely cold. But it does get wet! Kentucky averages about 45 inches (114 centimeters) of precipitation each year. Its neighbor Ohio averages only 37 inches (94 cm) of precipitation annually. Along its southern border with Tennessee, Kentucky gets even more annual rainfall than the rest of the state—about 50 inches (127 cm). Throughout the state, spring is the rainiest time of year; fall is the driest. Because winter temperatures are relatively mild, precipitation often falls in the form of rain or sleet instead of snow. About 12 inches (30 cm) of snow will fall in a typical Kentucky winter.

The combination of heavy precipitation and hilly ground makes a perfect recipe for flooding, especially in mountainous eastern Kentucky. The Ohio River has often overflowed its banks, sometimes damaging entire communities. More than 15 inches (38 cm) of rain fell across Kentucky in January 1937, sending the Ohio and Kentucky rivers pouring over their banks. Thousands of Louisville's residents were forced to evacuate in the flood of 1937, and Paducah had to be abandoned. In Frankfort, prisoners were move from the state prison when floodwaters moved in.

Earthquakes

You might not think of Kentucky as a likely spot for an earthquake, but it has experienced some of the most

A team of U.S. Army engineers built a floating sidewalk in Louisville to help evacuate residents and get food and supplies into the city during the flood of 1937.

powerful earthquakes ever felt in the United States. They struck in the winter of 1811–1812 along the New Madrid Fault Zone—an area that includes parts of Kentucky, Missouri, Arkansas, and Tennessee. People felt the four earthquakes from the Rocky Mountains to the Atlantic Ocean. **Seismologists** think the earthquakes may have caused the Mississippi River to flow backward for a brief period. Because this part of Kentucky was not heavily populated at the time, the property damage was only minor. Today, the area is home to much development and many people, and similar earthquakes would cause catastrophic damage.

WORD TO KNOW

seismologists *scientists who study earthquakes*

Kentucky National Park Areas

This map shows some of Kentucky's national parks, monuments, preserves, and other areas protected by the National Park Service.

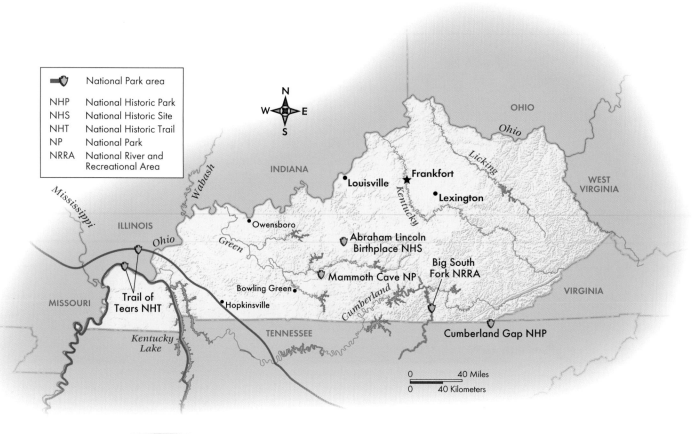

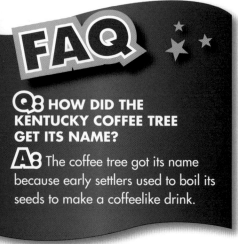

FAQ

Q: HOW DID THE KENTUCKY COFFEE TREE GET ITS NAME?

A: The coffee tree got its name because early settlers used to boil its seeds to make a coffeelike drink.

PLANT LIFE

A wide variety of plant life covers Kentucky. The state is home to 3,500 kinds of plants—3,000 kinds of flowering plants alone.

Named for leaves shaped like tulip petals, the tulip poplar grows to 100 feet (30 m) tall—that's about as tall as a five-story building. Much smaller, but equally impressive, is the watermeal. The smallest flowering

The goldenrod blooms in late summer throughout the state.

THE BLUEGRASS STATE

Bluegrass is known throughout the world as a symbol of Kentucky. But bluegrass is not native to Kentucky. For that matter, it's not even really blue. It's dark green. It may have gotten its name because people confused it with other grasses that had a more blue-green color. Bluegrass came to North America from England, where it was called smooth-stalked meadow grass. French traders traveling along the Great Lakes and the Ohio River in the 1600s and 1700s probably carried bluegrass seeds deep into the interior of North America. The grass spread quickly and was already common in Kentucky when white settlers began arriving.

As settlers cleared Kentucky's forests, bluegrass meadows took over in many places. It proved to be an excellent source of food for cattle and sheep. Because it stands up to heavy foot traffic, some Native Americans called it "white man's foot grass."

plant in the world, the watermeal grows in Kentucky's ponds and **sloughs**. These tiny, egg-shaped plants look like a green carpet floating on the water.

Kentucky gladecress is a wildflower that blooms early in the spring and exists only in Bullitt and Jefferson counties—and nowhere else in the world. Goldenrod, the official state flower, produces bright yellow flowers in fields and alongside roads in the late summer and fall. (You can also see goldenrod on the state flag.) Kentucky is home to more than 30 varieties of goldenrod.

WORD TO KNOW

sloughs *wet and marshy places, such as swamps*

The largest tree ever recorded in Kentucky is a sycamore found on Grassy Creek in Montgomery County. Its circumference, or the distance around the trunk, is 440 inches (1,118 cm), making it a national champion among sycamores.

Nearly half the state, or 12 million acres (4.9 million hectares), is forestland. Kentucky's forests are home to some gigantic trees. Kentucky coffee trees can grow as tall as 100 feet (30 m). They're found mostly in the Bluegrass region. The tallest tree in Kentucky is a yellow poplar in McCreary County that reaches 168 feet (51 m) tall.

ANIMAL LIFE

Hundreds of years ago, bison and other big mammals roamed Kentucky's forests. Wild turkeys were common, and passenger pigeons flew overhead in such numbers that they were said to darken the sky.

Kentucky's abundance of animals helped make it a favorite hunting ground for Native Americans. When the first white settlers came to Kentucky, they

A black bear and cubs in Kingdom Come State Park

commented on the great number of wild animals to be found. "We found everywhere abundance of wild beasts of every sort, through this vast forest," Daniel Boone recalled. But hunters killed so many animals that many species disappeared from Kentucky, including bison, wolves, and panthers. By the late 1800s, wild turkeys were mostly gone, as well.

Thanks to the efforts of conservationists, some species have been able to return to Kentucky. For example, wild turkeys began making a comeback and by 1993, more than 40,000 could be found in the state. Today, wild turkeys are found in every one of Kentucky's counties. Black bears had disappeared from the state by the 1900s, but today, they are found in eastern Kentucky. In the 1970s, bald eagles had disappeared from Kentucky, but as of the summer of 2007, there were at least 48 pairs living in the state. Kentucky is now home to 340 species of birds, 200 species of fish, 68 mammal species, and 100 species of amphibians and reptiles.

ENVIRONMENTAL ISSUES

Mining and forest clearing have severely affected the natural environment in parts of Kentucky. Finding a way to balance concern for the environment with the needs of industry is a major challenge facing the state. A recent University of Kentucky poll showed that more than nine out of every 10 people expressed medium to high concern about environmental issues in their communities.

Today, many Kentuckians are working to restore forestlands and find ways to mine that will not harm the environment. Kentucky has long been prized as a place of natural wonders. It will be up to Kentuckians to preserve those wonders.

KENTUCKY'S ENDANGERED SPECIES

Thirty-seven plant and animal species found in Kentucky are on the U.S. government's list of threatened and endangered species. Threatened and endangered species are plants or animals that may become extinct if action is not taken to save them. The scaleshell mussel and the American burying beetle are among the threatened and endangered species found in Kentucky. The state is also home to three species of bats that are on the federal endangered species list: the Indiana bat, the gray bat, and the Virginia big-eared bat. They find shelter in Kentucky's many caves.

Bald eagle

READ ABOUT

Paleo-Indians hunted together to take down prey as large as a mammoth.

c. 10,000 BCE

Paleo-Indians begin living in Kentucky

800–1000 BCE

People in Kentucky begin raising crops such as squash

Gaitskill Mound stone tablet

▲ c. 1000 BCE– 1000 CE

The Woodland peoples build burial mounds in Kentucky

CHAPTER TWO
FIRST PEOPLE

★

ABOUT 12,000 YEARS AGO, WHAT WE NOW KNOW AS KENTUCKY WAS A COLDER PLACE THAN IT IS TODAY. The area was home to mammoths that stood 14 feet (4.3 m) tall, ground sloths the size of oxen, and giant bison. The first Kentuckians hunted many of these animals for food, fur, and hides. We know these people as Paleo-Indians, which means ancient Indians.

▲ **1000**
People of the Mississippian culture begin growing corn

1100–1350
Native Americans start living in permanent villages along Kentucky's rivers

1750s
Shawnees live in a village called Eskippakithiki in Kentucky

Stone point for a spear

WORD TO KNOW

chert *a rock resembling flint*

Kentucky was once home to giant bison—even bigger than modern-day bison—that had horns spanning more than 6 feet (1.8 m).

PREHISTORIC KENTUCKY

Paleo-Indians were the first humans to live in North America. They came from Asia toward the end of the last ice age—between 15,000 and 12,000 years ago. They may have walked over a land link that once connected Siberia and Alaska. Eventually, they moved south and spread across the continent. Over time, some of them reached what we now know as Kentucky. They were highly skilled at fashioning sharp spear points from stone. Paleo-Indian toolmakers chipped away at pieces of hard rock called **chert** to create a very sharp, two-sided point shaped like the letter V. By attaching these points to the end of long wooden shafts, Paleo-Indians created spears.

How did prehistoric Kentuckians manage to kill such enormous animals using only spears? It turns out that those spears and stone points were combined in a very clever way. The stone points were designed to detach from the wooden shaft of the spear. Once a hunter had driven a spear into the animal's body, the hunter could pull out the shaft of the spear and reload it with another tip and stone point. This allowed hunters to wound the animal repeatedly and eventually bring the great beast down.

Much of what we know about these first Kentuckians comes from evidence they left behind at their hunting and toolmaking camps—remains of the animals they hunted and bits of the tools they used. Paleo-Indians lived on the move, and they left no traces of permanent settlements. They seldom stayed in one place for long. Researchers know this because their camps show no signs of housing or garbage piles—the usual clues that tell archaeologists that people had established permanent homes. Researchers have found traces of prehistoric camps or temporary settlements at more than 17,000 sites in Kentucky.

A CHANGE IN CLIMATE

As the last ice age ended and Kentucky's climate warmed, the largest animals were unable to survive. Their shaggy hides suited colder climates. With great mammals such as the mastodon driven to extinction, people began to rely on smaller animals for food. From about 8000 to 1000 BCE, people lived along Kentucky's rivers, where they caught fish and hunted for deer and smaller game. Some may have begun growing their own food by raising garden crops such as squash. They also stayed in one place more than the wandering Paleo-Indians did. Ancient sites near the Ohio River show signs of having been used all year long. In some places, people left enormous piles of mussel shells that they collected from rivers.

Around 1000 BCE, people began to farm more extensively. They grew squash, gourds, and sunflowers. They also made pottery that could be used to store and carry food. These Woodland peoples built hundreds of burial mounds in central and eastern Kentucky. High fences called **palisades** topped some; **moats** surrounded others.

A stone tablet found at the Gaitskill Mound

Native American Peoples
(Before European Contact)

This map shows the general area of Native American peoples before European settlers arrived.

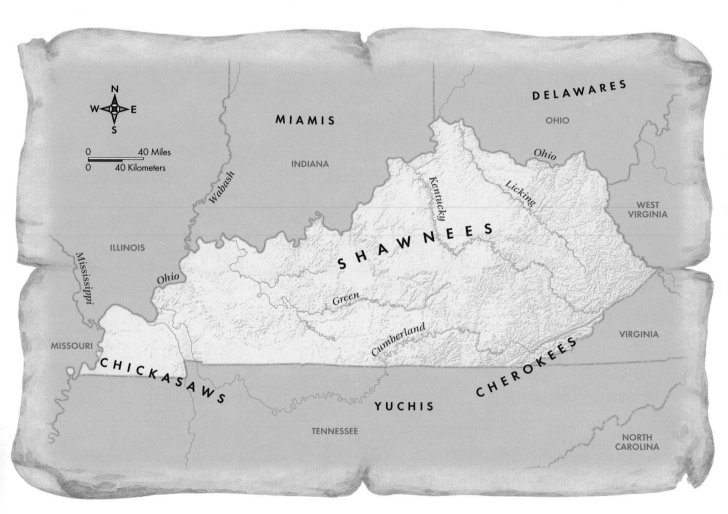

DELAWARES

MIAMIS

OHIO

INDIANA

Wabash

Ohio

Kentucky

Licking

WEST VIRGINIA

S H A W N E E S

ILLINOIS

Mississippi

Ohio

Green

Cumberland

VIRGINIA

MISSOURI

C H I C K A S A W S

C H E R O K E E S

YUCHIS

TENNESSEE

NORTH CAROLINA

0 — 40 Miles
0 — 40 Kilometers

FARMING COMES TO KENTUCKY

Even thousands of years ago, people in Kentucky had contact with people in other parts of North America. Woodland people made use of copper from the Great Lakes region and shells from the Gulf of Mexico. These items came to Kentucky through vast trade networks that crossed thousands of miles.

About 1,000 years ago, indigenous people began raising corn in Kentucky, marking the end of the Woodland period. Corn was first cultivated in Mexico, and people in other parts of the Americas soon started growing it as well. Because it was easy to grow, harvest, and store, it became a valuable crop. As farming became more important to people living in Kentucky, they increasingly settled in permanent villages.

Seven hundred years ago, Wickliffe Mounds State Historic Site was one such village. Several hundred people lived there from about 1100 to about 1350, build-

Clay pottery from the Mississippian culture portray both male and female figures.

WORDS TO KNOW

bluff *a high, steep bank*

stockades *enclosures of posts designed to protect against attack*

ing homes and earthen mounds around a central plaza on a **bluff** along the Mississippi River. The mounds may have been places of worship. Villagers farmed the fertile soil along the river. They also traveled on the river to trade with people hundreds of miles away.

People of the Mississippian culture built other villages and towns along the major rivers in western and southern Kentucky. Much like the design of the settlement at the Wickliffe site, a typical Mississippian village had a central plaza surrounded by houses and other buildings, with farm fields nearby. Some of these settlements included large mounds or pyramids that may have been used as places of worship. These villages were among hundreds that stretched across much of what is now the southeastern United States.

In eastern Kentucky, a different farming culture developed, also about 1,000 years ago. Its people lived in villages often circular in shape and sometimes surrounded by **stockades**. Scholars call it the Fort Ancient culture. Some historians believe that corn made up as much as half of their diet.

The Mississippian and Fort Ancient cultures disappeared before the first European explorers arrived in Kentucky. Those cultures were probably the ancestors of the Native peoples who lived or hunted in Kentucky when Europeans arrived.

The Shawnee, Cherokee, and Chickasaw people all lived or hunted in parts of Kentucky. Members of many other groups—including the Delaware,

Picture Yourself . . .

Playing Games in a Fort Ancient Village

Have you ever competed with your friends to see who could come closest to hitting a target? If you grew up in a Fort Ancient village, you would have played games a lot like that. You and your friends would meet in the central plaza of the village, which you would use as your playing field. You'd gather a collection of smooth, rounded, disk-shaped stones to play *chunkey* (or *chunkee*). One of you would roll a disk along the ground, while the others took aim with poles, trying to knock it down. The one who came closest to the disk or knocked it down was the winner.

Piankashaw, and Yuchi—also visited Kentucky to hunt, live, or trade. The Warriors' Path, which ran between the Ohio River and the Cumberland Gap, connected Shawnee towns near the Ohio River with Cherokee lands in the Appalachian Mountains. Trails like this, which Indians followed to reach distant hunting grounds or to trade with faraway tribes, crisscrossed Kentucky.

SHAWNEES

Eskippakithiki, a Shawnee village, was one of the last Native settlements in Kentucky. Located in present-day Clark County, Eskippakithiki was protected by a stockade and surrounded by farmland. Shawnee women did the farmwork, raising corn, beans, squash, and other crops. They also tapped maple trees for the sap that they made into syrup. Shawnee families lived in **longhouses** made of wood frames covered in animal skins. At the center of each village was a council house used for community meetings.

Shawnee women tapped maple trees and cooked the sap to make syrup and sugar during the winter months.

WORD TO KNOW

longhouses *long buildings made and used by a Native American community*

A reconstruction of a Shawnee village

Life for Shawnee children was busy. Girls helped their mothers tend the crops, gather edible wild plants, and prepare food. They also learned to make clothes using deerskins and other materials from the natural world. Boys trained to become hunters and warriors. They went through a ritual called a vision quest. Part of the vision quest involved rising at dawn to perform demanding physical challenges. They might have to run naked through a forest until they reached a pond or stream. Then they had to dive into the frigid water. This might continue for several days. Finally, the boy would be told to dive to the bottom of the pond and grab the first object he could reach. This would become his "power object," and he would keep it with him for protection and spiritual guidance.

In the fall and winter months, Shawnees left their villages to hunt. As they traveled in search of game, they lived in small dwellings that could be easily assembled, taken down, and carried to another location. Shawnee men hunted and defended their lands in northern and eastern Kentucky.

CHEROKEES

The traditional homeland of the Cherokee people extended along the Appalachian Mountains and included the southeastern corner of Kentucky. They were expert farmers, and they built towns around a central square. At the center of some towns were homes for leaders of the community, which were built atop mounds. Cherokee towns often included a large council house for meetings.

CHICKASAWS

The southwestern corner of Kentucky was Chickasaw territory. Each Chickasaw family owned two houses: a rectangular summer house with a wood frame covered with mats of grass or bark, and a circular winter house made of pine logs. Each Chickasaw village maintained a sacred fire. In the spring, villagers put out the sacred fire and kindled a new one that would serve for the rest of the year. Each household would light its fires from the sacred fire.

Chickasaws were known for being among the tallest of the Native Americans. Chickasaw men were often well over 6 feet (183 cm) tall. Newborn Chickasaw infants were laid down to sleep on their backs, so that the backs of their heads became flat as they grew. Chickasaws also covered their bodies with many tattoos.

Other Native peoples played a part in Kentucky's past. Miamis, Mingos, and Senecas are also among those who spent time in Kentucky. This rich Indian heritage would be all but lost in the 1800s.

READ ABOUT

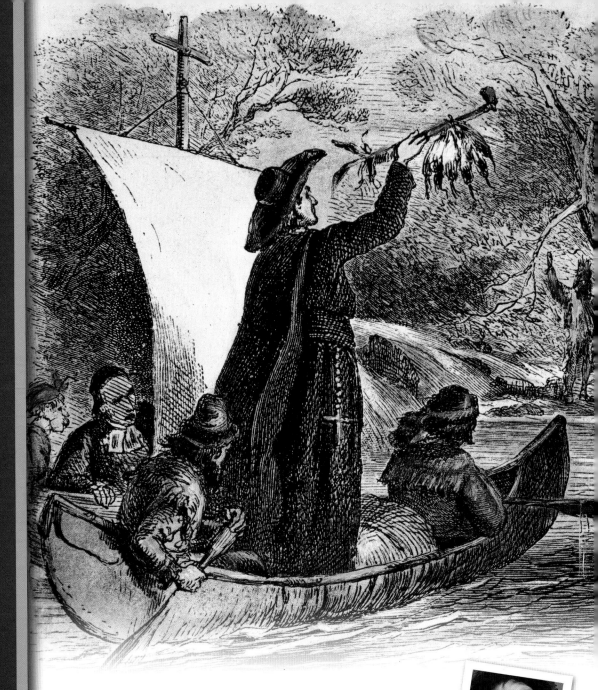

Jacques Marquette carried a decorative pipe as a sign of peace while he explored the Mississippi River in 1673.

1673
Jacques Marquette explores the Mississippi River

1774
James Harrod leads settlers into Kentucky

1775 ▶
Daniel Boone widens the Wilderness Road from the Cumberland Gap into Kentucky

CHAPTER THREE

EXPLORATION AND SETTLEMENT

★

F OR CENTURIES, THE RIVERS THAT FLOW THROUGH AND AROUND KENTUCKY SERVED AS NATURAL HIGHWAYS FOR NATIVE AMERICANS. Like them, European explorers traveled deep into North America by canoe. The first Europeans to enter Kentucky were French explorers from settlements in Canada. They paddled along the Mississippi and Ohio rivers in the 1600s and 1700s.

1776

The Virginia legislature creates Kentucky County

1792 ▶

The constitutional convention permits slavery, and Kentucky becomes the 15th state

1790–1800

Thousands of settlers enter Kentucky through the Cumberland Gap

EARLY EUROPEAN EXPLORERS

In 1673, a French missionary named Jacques Marquette and a group of explorers, including Canadian Louis Jolliet, paddled down the Mississippi River past what is now western Kentucky. Marquette noted the Shawnee towns along the Ohio River, but he didn't stay long enough to learn much about the Shawnee people or about Kentucky. Then, in 1749, a French soldier named Pierre-Joseph Celoron de Bienville explored along the Ohio River. At the junction of the Ohio and the Big Sandy rivers in northeastern Kentucky, he buried lead plates that stated France's claim to the region.

France was not the only European nation interested in Kentucky. English colonists along the Atlantic coast sought to push west and settle the land on the other side of the Appalachian Mountains. Leaders of the English colony in Virginia claimed Kentucky as theirs.

Both the French and the English ignored the fact that Native Americans had been living on the land for centuries. By the mid-1700s, most Indians were struggling to survive. European diseases were spreading rapidly through Native populations that had no immunities to them. In many cases, these diseases spread from group to group, reaching some Native peoples even before they had contact with Europeans. By the time white settlers began pouring into Kentucky in the late 1700s, many Native people had died from these diseases.

In 1750, the Loyal Land Company of Virginia sent Thomas Walker, a doctor and surveyor, to explore the land west of the Appalachian Mountains. The company hoped to establish the first European settlements in Kentucky. Traveling with five other men, Walker followed a passage through the rugged mountains that divide Kentucky from Virginia. He named it the Cumberland

SEE IT HERE!

DR. THOMAS WALKER STATE HISTORIC SITE

Thomas Walker's expedition across the Appalachian Mountains lasted four months. He and his group built a cabin near present-day Barbourville, Kentucky, where they stayed for about a week. They pushed north and crossed the Kentucky River before returning to Virginia. Visitors can see a replica of Walker's tiny cabin at the Dr. Thomas Walker State Historic Site in Barbourville.

European Exploration of Kentucky

The colored arrows on this map show the routes taken by explorers between 1673 and 1775.

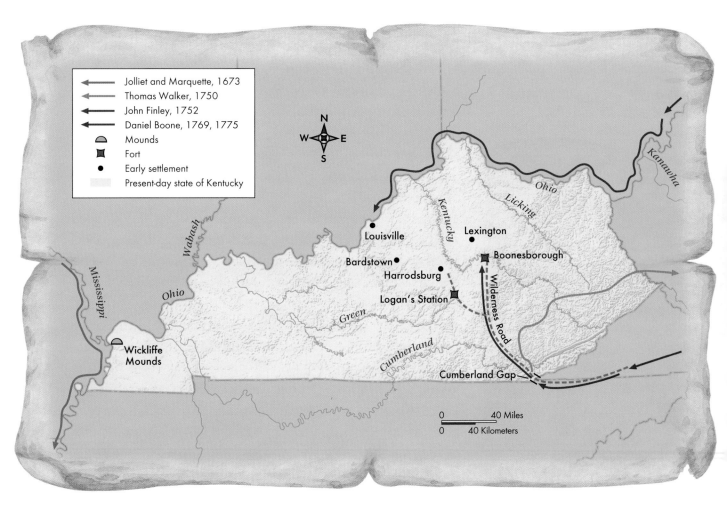

Gap in honor of the Duke of Cumberland, an English general and nobleman. Although Native Americans had been traveling through the gap for centuries, Walker was the first European to record its existence. In the process, he helped open a route for early white and black settlers to follow into Kentucky. In the years ahead, thousands of new Kentuckians would enter through the gap.

LONG HUNTERS

People from Virginia and other English colonies followed Walker's route through the Cumberland Gap into Kentucky. Hunters crossed the mountains on hunting expeditions that lasted for months. Because their hunts kept them away from home for so long, they were called "long hunters." Merchants paid high prices for animal **pelts** that could be made into gloves, hats, and other items. In Kentucky, hunters found abundant deer, bison, and other animals. On a single trip, a group of hunters could gather thousands of animal skins.

Risks were high for the hunters, however. They faced many hardships, including bad weather and dangerous river crossings. A whole season's work could be lost in one disastrous day. In 1769, a group of hunters left a message on a Kentucky poplar tree: "2,300 deer skins lost. Ruination by God." The hunters also clashed with Native Americans protecting their traditional hunting grounds.

Daniel Boone was one of the greatest long hunters to go to Kentucky. Though he had first visited there in 1767, he came from North Carolina with a small party of hunters to Kentucky in 1769 and explored much more of the region. He stayed and hunted for two years, sending his skins back east with his brother Squire. When Boone went back to North Carolina, he vowed to return one day to Kentucky and make a home there. He wrote, "I returned home to my family with a determination to bring them as soon as possible to live in Kentucky, which I esteemed a second paradise."

When the first white hunters began moving into Kentucky, they found some 25 million acres (10 mil-

WORD TO KNOW

pelts *animal skins covered in fur*

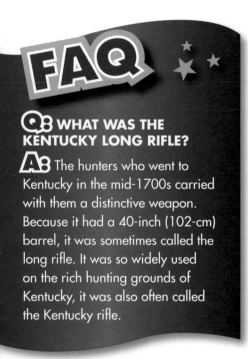

Q8 WHAT WAS THE KENTUCKY LONG RIFLE?

A8 The hunters who went to Kentucky in the mid-1700s carried with them a distinctive weapon. Because it had a 40-inch (102-cm) barrel, it was sometimes called the long rifle. It was so widely used on the rich hunting grounds of Kentucky, it was also often called the Kentucky rifle.

lion ha) of forest. The dense woods not only provided habitat for wild game but also produced food and medicine for Kentuckians. Native Americans taught white settlers to make a food called pemmican by mixing berries with animal fat. Kentuckians also learned to use the roots of trees such as black cherries and plants such as goldenseal to treat everything from stomachaches to eye problems. Soon Kentucky's forests would provide materials for homes, fences, and furnishings for thousands of new settlers.

A hunter dressed in buckskin clothing carries a turkey through the forest in winter.

FIRST EUROPEAN SETTLEMENTS

News spread about Kentucky's rich forests, abundant wildlife, and lush meadows. As populations grew in the colonies along the Atlantic coast, many people talked of moving west and starting new lives in Kentucky.

In 1774, James Harrod led a group of 31 men down the Ohio River, then up the Kentucky River. In present-day Mercer County, they began building cabins. They had to leave the site because of conflicts with Native Americans, but they came back the next year even more determined to build a fort and more homes. The settlement would grow into the town of Harrodsburg.

In 1775, Boone returned to Kentucky to settle. The Transylvania Land Company hired him to cut a road from the mountains to the fertile Bluegrass region. Leading a group of about 30 men and two women, Boone cut a path that became known as the Wilderness Road. It was slow, difficult work cutting down trees, clearing rocks, and finding safe places to cross swift rivers. When they reached the Kentucky River, they built a fort. The settlement that grew up around the fort became known as Boonesborough.

Many of the first European settlers brought African slaves to Kentucky. An African American woman, whose name was not recorded, was among the first group of people to arrive at Boonesborough. Slaves cleared fields for farming and tended crops. During Indian attacks, slaves often helped defend the forts. By 1777, these African men and women made up 10 percent of the first settlers in this Native American land.

THE REVOLUTIONARY WAR

As settlers were streaming into Kentucky, the young United States was fighting to win its independence from Great Britain. When the American Revolutionary War

MINI-BIO

DANIEL BOONE: LEGENDARY FRONTIERSMAN

Daniel Boone (1734–1820) was born in Berks County, Pennsylvania. After making several hunting trips to Kentucky, he led 30 people who cut a road from the mountains into the heart of Kentucky in 1775. There he helped establish Boonesborough, one of the first white settlements in Kentucky. In 1778, he was captured by a group of Shawnee warriors and was adopted by their chief, Blackfish. Five months later, he escaped and returned to Boonesborough. This was just one of the many adventures recounted in John Filson's book, *The Discovery, Settlement and Present State of Kentucke*, published in 1784. The book helped make Boone famous. Boone later represented the Kentucky settlements in the Virginia legislature. In 1799, he moved to Missouri, where he served as a local official. He died there in 1820. In 1845, his remains were relocated to a cemetery in Frankfort, Kentucky.

? Want to know more? See http://www.americanwest.com/pages/boone.htm

(1775–1783) broke out, British authorities encouraged Native Americans in Kentucky and elsewhere along the frontier to attack new settlements. Native Americans feared that more and more settlers would push west, taking lands where they lived or hunted. With British help, they hoped to drive out the settlers, who lived in groups of small, **isolated** communities numbering not more than a few hundred people. These tiny Kentucky settlements came under frequent attack. Some settlers left and returned to more heavily populated areas east of the Appalachian Mountains.

Although Kentucky was part of the new state of Virginia, its people could not depend on help from its government. With the American Revolution raging, Virginia authorities could not spare **militia** forces to help protect Kentucky settlements.

For safety, settlers often built their cabins in clusters called stations. Conflicts with Indians often drove settlers into the forts at Harrodsburg or Boonesborough for protection. There they took shelter and banded together with other families to defend against attacks. Boonesborough had a wood stockade that encircled 20 cabins, and a stream ran through the fort, providing fresh water. With settlers crowded into the fort, however, conditions often became unhealthy. A visitor to Boonesborough wrote of the "dirt and filth of the fort" washing into the stream and polluting the water. Food often became scarce during hard winters. Another visitor wrote that people in Boonesborough had "no bred [sic], no salt, no vegetables, no fruit of any kind."

SHAWNEE LEADER

Blackfish (?–1779) was a leader of the Chalahgawtha (or Chillicothe) Shawnee, one group of the Shawnee people. In 1778, to avenge the murder of a Shawnee chief named Cornstalk by white settlers, he led about 120 Shawnee warriors on a raid near Boonesborough, capturing Daniel Boone and 30 other Kentucky settlers. Blackfish returned with his captives to the Shawnee village of Chillicothe, in what is now Ohio. Blackfish adopted Boone and named him Shel-to-wee, or Big Turtle. Boone eventually escaped to Boonesborough. In 1779, Blackfish was wounded in a battle with white Kentucky settlers and died as a result of his injuries.

WORDS TO KNOW

isolated *set apart from others*

militia *an army made up of citizens trained to serve as soldiers in an emergency*

A view of Fort Boonesborough as it appeared in 1778

George Rogers Clark and other leaders in Kentucky hoped to gain support and supplies from Virginia to help defend the new communities. Clark appealed to the Virginia state legislature to recognize Kentucky as a county. Legislators agreed, creating Kentucky County on December 31, 1776. Clark became a leader of the Kentucky militia, and his troops captured several British forts across the Ohio River from Kentucky. But even after the American Revolution ended in 1783, Indian attacks continued as Native Americans sought to stop the flow of white and black settlers into Kentucky.

Kentucky: The Road to Statehood
(1777–1792)

This map shows the original state of Virginia and the area (outlined in orange) that became the state of Kentucky in 1792.

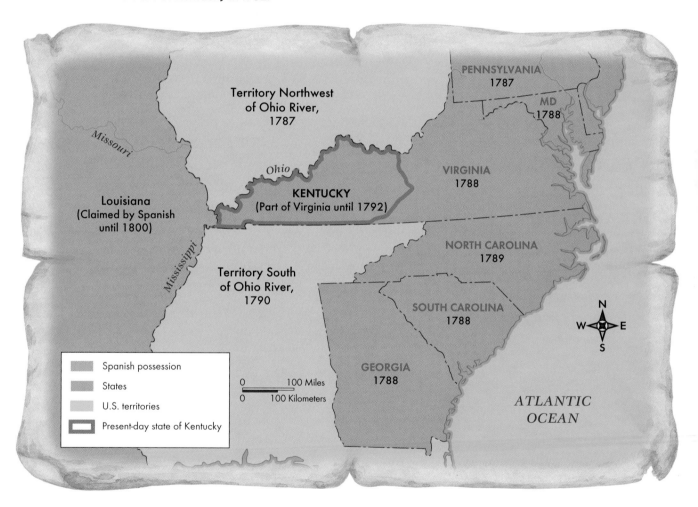

BECOMING A STATE

Still under Virginia's control, Kentuckians felt increasingly dissatisfied with the state government. To reach the Virginia state legislature or high courts, Kentuckians had to make the long journey east over the mountains. Because of their isolation, they enjoyed few services such as regular mail delivery. Most of all, Kentuckians believed that Virginia's leaders didn't understand their lives or their concerns.

Through the 1780s and 1790s, Kentucky's population grew large enough to encourage its leaders to discuss plans for statehood. By 1790, Kentucky claimed a population of 73,677, including 11,830 slaves and 114 free black people. Residents began the complicated process of seeking political separation from Virginia.

Between 1784 and 1792, Kentuckians held 10 conventions to discuss plans for becoming a separate state. One contentious issue was slavery, which had been a part of life in Kentucky since the earliest days of white settlement. Kentucky ministers led the fight against slavery in the 1792 **constitutional** convention. But many Kentuckians had come from southern states that allowed slavery. In its 1792 constitution, Kentucky permitted slavery. On June 1, 1792, Kentucky entered the Union as the 15th state.

GETTING TO KENTUCKY

In the late 1700s, large numbers of people began moving to Kentucky seeking better lives. In 1784, Kentucky explorer and author John Filson wrote that "numbers are daily arriving and, multitudes expected this fall." Filson predicted that Kentucky would become "exceedingly populous in a short time." He was right. Between 1790 and 1800, Kentucky's population grew from about 73,000 to 220,955. Settlers came because they had heard that land was readily available. Many hoped that making a new start in a "new" land would make them wealthy and successful.

WORD TO KNOW

constitutional *relating to a written document that states the main principles around which a political body will be organized to guide its government*

Settlers moving from the east to Kentucky faced obstacles, starting with the Appalachian Mountains. This mountain range, stretching from Maine to Georgia, forms a natural wall dividing Kentucky from its eastern neighbors. Daniel Boone's Wilderness Road, which ran from the Cumberland Gap to the Bluegrass region of Kentucky, passed over rugged terrain. Indians protecting their land sometimes attacked travelers. So did thieves who struck on the lonely trails. At least four major rivers had to be crossed, and each crossing meant the risk of a disastrous accident.

For poor travelers, making the trip in winter could prove fatal. One traveler recalled seeing "men, women and children" walking through mountain passes in icy weather "without Shoe or Stocking." Wealthier settlers could choose another route. Many bought passage aboard flatboats that floated down the Ohio River from western Pennsylvania into Kentucky. Flatboats, named for their flat bottoms, included a cabin that could shelter families, their **livestock**, and all their possessions. Oarsmen propelled the boats, which traveled as far as 100 miles (161 km) in a day. Settlers trudging across the mountains could only dream of making that kind of progress.

Other new arrivals in Kentucky had no choice about how or where they would move. White settlers continued to bring thousands of black slaves to Kentucky.

Picture Yourself . . .

Doing Chores on the Frontier

Do you have chores to do around your house? Compare them to the list of jobs Daniel Drake had as a boy living in Mason County, Kentucky, in the late 1700s. They included: taking care of his younger brothers and sisters, grating and pounding corn to make cornmeal, bringing water home in buckets from a distant spring, milking the family cow, chopping wood for the fireplace, helping his mother wash clothes (they used rainwater collected in washtubs and buckets), and hanging wet clothes to dry on a fence. Drake grew up to become a doctor and wrote about his childhood labors in a book published in 1870 called *Pioneer Life in Kentucky, 1785–1800: A Series of Reminiscential Letters from Daniel Drake, MD of Cincinnati to His Children.*

WORD TO KNOW

livestock *farm animals such as cows and hogs*

44

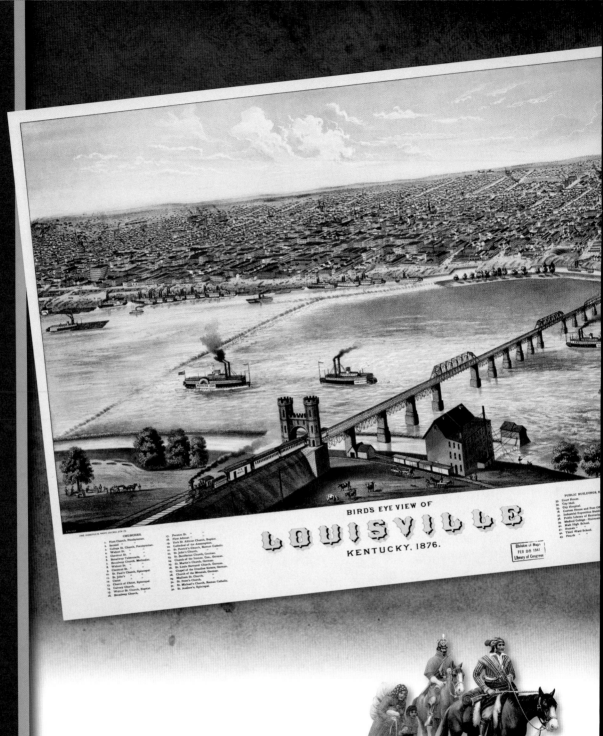

BIRD'S EYE VIEW OF
LOUISVILLE
KENTUCKY, 1876.

Division of Maps
FEB 28 1941
Library of Congress

A map of
Louisville shows
how it appeared
in 1876 along
the Ohio River.

1812–1815
*More than 25,000
Kentuckians fight in the
War of 1812*

1818
*The Chickasaw
are forced to give
up their land in
Kentucky*

1838 ▲
*The U.S. government
orders the Cherokee to
leave their homeland in the
Appalachian Mountains*

GROWTH AND CHANGE

K ENTUCKY WAS STILL A YOUNG STATE AT THE START OF THE 1800s, BUT ITS CITIES WERE EXPANDING. Louisville's location on the Ohio River would help make it a key point for commerce and shipping. Lexington, with its theater, bookstores, library, and music, was considered a center for culture. Frankfort became Kentucky's capital.

1845 ▶
Cassius M. Clay starts the True American newspaper

1862
Civil War battles are fought at Richmond and Perryville

1870–1900
Industry expands in Kentucky

Congressman Henry Clay

WAR OF 1812

In national politics, Henry Clay, a congressman from Kentucky, became one of the most powerful U.S. leaders during the first few decades of the 1800s. He led a group of congressmen called War Hawks, who blamed Great Britain for encouraging Native Americans to attack frontier settlements in Kentucky and elsewhere. Clay helped lead the move to declare war against Great Britain, launching the War of 1812. More than 25,000 Kentuckians fought in the war, earning themselves a reputation for fierceness.

WORK IN EARLY KENTUCKY

As Kentucky grew, most newcomers to the state farmed. Clearing wilderness for farm fields was the first and most important job for newcomers. Trees had to be chopped down, rocks removed, and soil prepared. With the help of neighbors, a farmer could build a simple log cabin in less than a week. Many cabins included lofts, which were partial second floors tucked in just below a slanted roof. Lofts typically served as children's sleeping quarters.

Farmers usually planted corn first. It fed both their families and their pigs and other livestock. Many farmers also planted wheat. Children played important roles on small farms. Families depended on them to help with the never-ending farm chores. Girls helped their mothers with household tasks, and boys helped their fathers tend fields and care for farm equipment.

In addition to feeding their families, farmers also raised crops to sell. Farmers used Kentucky's many rivers to connect to the Ohio and Mississippi rivers and transport their cash crops to markets as far away as New Orleans. Tobacco was Kentucky's first big cash

Many farm girls' duties often included tending cattle.

crop. Many of Kentucky's early settlers had come from Virginia and Maryland, where tobacco grew. They found it flourished in Kentucky, too.

Another key crop in early Kentucky was hemp, a source of fiber for making ropes and durable cloth. The first hemp crop was planted in Kentucky in 1775, and Kentucky soon became a major hemp producer.

Since producing hemp required a great deal of manual labor, enslaved people often were sent to work on hemp farms. In its first decade as a state, the number of slaves in Kentucky rapidly increased. Most lived in the Bluegrass region, where big farms depended on slave labor. Slaves also served in white households, the skilled trades, and transportation. By 1830, almost one in four Kentuckians was enslaved. These African American men, women, and children frequently had to endure cruel treatment and poor living conditions. Their homes were often small, crowded cabins stocked only with crude furniture.

Not every black person in Kentucky lived in slavery. Scattered about the state were a few small communities of free black people. In country towns and in cities such as Lexington and Louisville, they organized churches and schools. In 1830, nearly 5,000 free blacks lived in Kentucky (compared to more than 165,000 slaves). Though called free, they were granted few rights that white people enjoyed. Free blacks were denied the right to vote, hold office, or serve on juries. They had to carry "free papers" at all times to identify themselves as free blacks. And they could be arrested and punished harshly for even minor offenses.

THE TRAIL OF TEARS

White settlers gobbled up Kentucky's land, leaving less and less space for the original Kentuckians. Shawnees had fought back against the first wave of white settlers to move into Kentucky, but more and more settlers soon drove them out. Chickasaws, known among other Native Americans as fierce warriors, defended their land in Kentucky into the 1800s. Under pressure from white settlers, Chickasaws gave up their Kentucky land in the Jackson Purchase of 1818 and eventually resettled in what is now Oklahoma.

In 1838, the U.S. government ordered the removal of the Cherokees from their mountain homelands. About 19,000 Cherokees traveled more than 1,000 miles (1,609 km)—some by boat, others on foot—to

CHEROKEE LEADER

Whitepath (?–1839) led the Cherokee people during times of great change. In the early 1800s, as more and more white settlers arrived, many Cherokee were adopting "white" traditions and ways of life. Whitepath urged his people to hold fast to their traditions. When the U.S. government ordered the Cherokee to leave their homes in 1838, Whitepath helped lead them west on the brutal journey to their new home. He did not survive the Trail of Tears. He died in 1839 near Hopkinsville, Kentucky. There the Trail of Tears Commemorative Park marks his final resting place.

Many Cherokees did not survive the hard journey on the Trail of Tears.

settle in what is now Oklahoma. Because of the harsh conditions they encountered, about 4,000 Cherokees died along the way. Their journey became known as the Trail of Tears.

THE ANTISLAVERY MOVEMENT

Kentucky was a significant battleground in the national debate over slavery because of its location, on the border between slave states (Virginia to the east, Tennessee to the south, and Missouri to the west) and Free States (Illinois, Indiana, and Ohio to the north). Kentucky had an antislavery society in 1807 and dozens more a generation later. Black Kentuckians, both free and enslaved, took action to battle slavery.

Whether they worked on plantations, in stables, or in cities, enslaved men and women tried to escape their masters. Many slaves tried to escape to freedom across

ESCAPE!

On a Sunday in August 1848, as many as 75 armed African Americans in Fayette County began making their way toward the Ohio River in a bid for freedom. They were led by three enslaved men named Shadrack, Henry, and Prestley, and their guide was Patrick Doyle, a white student from Centre College. After a reward of $5,000 was offered for their capture, a posse of more than 100 men raced after them. Two furious battles were fought before the posse captured most of the rebels. Their three leaders were executed, and Doyle was sentenced to 20 years in prison. Even as the executions took place, 40 enslaved people in Woodford County made another attempt, only to be discovered and stopped.

the Ohio River, Kentucky's northern border, where antislavery activists would shelter runaway slaves. In 1848, near Lexington, 55 to 75 escaping slaves battled with state militia as they tried to make their way north to freedom. Most were recaptured in one of the largest slave uprisings ever in the United States.

One of slavery's fiercest opponents was a Kentucky lawyer and newspaper publisher named Cassius M. Clay. Born in 1810 to a slaveholding family in Madison County, Clay became disgusted with slavery, and in 1845, he began publishing the *True American,* an antislavery newspaper in Lexington. This infuriated his foes, who, in his absence, dismantled his press and shipped it to Ohio. In 1851, the unstoppable Clay ran for governor of Kentucky on a pledge to end slavery. Although he was defeated, he would later become a leader of the new Republican Party and continue to fight against slavery.

As conflict between Northern and Southern states began to divide the nation, Kentucky senator Henry Clay

Cassius M. Clay

led Congress in the search for a resolution. He worked for years to avoid a conflict over slavery and proposed the Compromise of 1850, a series of acts that aimed to satisfy both proslavery and antislavery leaders and to avoid a civil war. Another Kentuckian active on the national political scene was John J. Crittenden. In December 1860, as Confederate (Southern) and Union (Northern) forces prepared for war, he stepped forward with a compromise of his own. But it was rejected, and in April 1861, the Civil War began. Kentucky was soon torn by the bitter conflict.

MINI-BIO

JAMES G. BIRNEY: ANTISLAVERY PUBLISHER

James G. Birney (1792–1857) was born in Danville to a wealthy slaveholding family. But he came to hate slavery, and in 1834, he freed his own slaves. In 1835, he organized the Kentucky Anti-Slavery Society. The following year, he was forced to flee to Ohio. In Cincinnati, Ohio, he published an antislavery newspaper. In 1836, proslavery mobs tore his office apart and threw his press in the river, while the mayor watched approvingly and no police appeared. Birney eventually moved to New York, where he became a leading abolitionist. He pledged to fight "until slavery shall be exterminated, or liberty destroyed."

❓ **Want to know more?** See www.nndb.com/people/258/000050108/

THE ISSUE OF SLAVERY

Kentucky produced some of the major figures involved in the national clash over slavery. Both Abraham Lincoln and Jefferson Davis were born in Kentucky. Onetime slaveholder Cassius M. Clay turned against the system in its early days. James G. Birney, a wealthy former slaveholder, became the Liberty Party's first presidential candidate in 1840 and again in 1844. Kentucky produced the two figures who pushed for compromise in the U.S. Senate on the issue: Senators Henry Clay and John Crittenden.

Fugitive slaves from Kentucky made their own mark. Henry Bibb escaped from slavery to become a lecturer and editor of *Voice of the Fugitive*. Josiah Henson furnished information to Harriet Beecher Stowe for her influential novel *Uncle Tom's Cabin*, and may have served as a model for its Uncle Tom character. And William Wells Brown was among the country's first black playwrights, an untiring speaker for the antislavery cause, and a successful "conductor" on the Underground Railroad—the secret network of people who helped slaves escape to freedom.

A Confederate cavalry raids a small village in 1862.

U.S. president Abraham Lincoln and Confederate president Jefferson Davis were both born in Kentucky. Lincoln was born in 1809 near Hodgenville. Less than a year before, and only about 100 miles (161 km) away, Davis was born, near Fairview.

THE CIVIL WAR

Kentucky was so important to Union victory in the Civil War that President Abraham Lincoln was reported to have said that he hoped God was on his side, but he really needed Kentucky. Kentucky was strategically significant, with a border that ran along the Ohio River for almost 500 miles (805 km) and two rivers, the Cumberland and Tennessee, that led deep into the South. Both sides also wanted to tap into Kentucky's resources of manpower and manufacturing.

But Kentucky was deeply split, and its governor rejected both Confederate and Union calls for troops. Lincoln promised to keep Union troops out of the state if Kentucky did not act against the United States. When Confederates invaded Kentucky, the state legislature became strongly pro-Union and declared "the invaders must be expelled." Union troops moved in to occupy parts of Kentucky. By 1862, 35,000 Confederates occupied southwest Kentucky and 50,000 Union troops occupied the rest of the state.

The two sides fought bloody battles at Richmond and Perryville in 1862. At Perryville, 7,700 men were killed or wounded. Neither side won a clear victory, but the Confederates had to retreat. Perryville was the last major battle of the war in Kentucky. But raids and violence continued for three more years until the Confederacy's final defeat in 1865. Throughout the war, Kentuckians suffered as violent bands of outlaws stole their livestock, damaged their property, and murdered civilians.

The Civil War spelled the end of slavery in Kentucky. In the confusion of the war, many slaves escaped. Some joined the Union army to help fight against the Confederacy. At the war's end, the 13th Amendment to the U.S. Constitution freed all slaves in the United States.

AFTER THE WAR

Even after the war's end, bitterness and violence continued to grip Kentucky. The state's **economy** had been badly damaged by the war. Kentuckians had always sold farm products and other goods to markets in the South, but the war left many Southerners too poor to afford Kentucky's products.

Former slaves were a frequent target of violent racist groups. In 1871, black citizens of Frankfort petitioned the U.S. Congress for relief. They detailed 116 murders by the Ku Klux Klan and repeated "bloody deeds" against schools, churches, and families of both races who stood up for equality. "They refuse to allow us to testify in state Courts where a white man is concerned," they wrote, and requested laws "that will protect us" and "enable us to exercise the rights of citizens." The petition ended with a question, "how long is this state of things to last?"

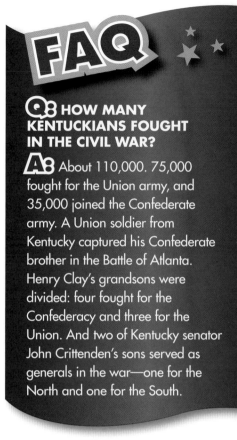

Q3 HOW MANY KENTUCKIANS FOUGHT IN THE CIVIL WAR?

A3 About 110,000. 75,000 fought for the Union army, and 35,000 joined the Confederate army. A Union soldier from Kentucky captured his Confederate brother in the Battle of Atlanta. Henry Clay's grandsons were divided: four fought for the Confederacy and three for the Union. And two of Kentucky senator John Crittenden's sons served as generals in the war—one for the North and one for the South.

WORD TO KNOW

economy *the system of producing and consuming goods and services in a community*

THE HATFIELDS AND MCCOYS

In the late 1800s, feuds—violent clashes between rival families—rocked the mountain regions of eastern Kentucky. The best-known of these feuds was between the Hatfields and the McCoys along the border between West Virginia and Kentucky. No one knows for sure what started the feud. Some say it was a dispute over a stolen pig; others say the fight dated back to disagreements related to the Civil War. But in the 1880s and 1890s, members of the two clans repeatedly attacked and killed each other. Before law enforcement could put an end to the violence, between 12 and 20 deaths were blamed on the feud.

WORD TO KNOW

distilleries *places where alcoholic products such as whiskey are produced*

The 15th Amendment to the U.S. Constitution established the rights of black men to vote. However, unfair local voting regulations and the threat of violence kept many black people from voting. In Kentucky and elsewhere, blacks would have to continue to fight against injustice and discrimination.

Some progress on other issues was made in the years after the war. In 1865, Kentucky's General Assembly created a state university at Lexington that provided greater opportunities for education. And in 1866, Berea College opened its doors to both white and black students, making it the first interracial college in the South.

Industry in Kentucky expanded after the war. Employment in the iron, timber, and other industries increased by 200 percent between 1870 and 1900. To serve industry, new roads and railway lines spread across the state. Kentucky had 1,000 miles (1,609 km) of railroads in 1870; by 1900, its railroad mileage had grown to 3,060 (4,925 km).

Immigrants from Germany and Ireland, who had first come to Kentucky in large numbers in the 1840s, continued to arrive in Louisville and other cities. Their work helped Kentucky industries thrive. Thanks in part to the arrival of immigrants, Louisville's population doubled to more than 200,000 between 1870 and 1900. While the immigrant population rose, Kentucky's black population began to fall during the Great Migration of the early 1900s, when thousands of black people moved to the northern cities of the United States.

An old Kentucky tradition became a booming business after the Civil War. For years, Kentucky farmers had been turning their grain into bourbon whiskey and selling it at market. Hundreds of whiskey **distilleries** sprang up around Kentucky in the late 1800s. But even as Kentucky became famous for its bourbon, some women's groups and religious leaders rose up in opposition to alcohol.

Horse racing and horse breeding had been part of life in Kentucky since the late 18th century. Farms in the Bluegrass region had become famous for producing superior racehorses. One visitor to Kentucky noted: "Horses are raised in great numbers and of the noblest kinds. A handsome horse is the highest pride of a Kentuckian; and common farmers own from ten to fifty."

In 1875, the first Kentucky Derby drew a crowd of 10,000 people to Churchill Downs in Louisville to see jockey Oliver Lewis ride Aristides to victory. Lewis was one of 14 African American jockeys in that first race. Between 1875 and 1902, African American jockeys won 15 of the 28 Kentucky Derby races. The Kentucky Derby, run each May, became the best-known symbol of Kentucky horse racing.

In 1882, Kentucky-born African American Isaac Murphy became the first jockey to win the Kentucky Derby three times. He was the greatest jockey of the 19th century.

The field races down the homestretch at the 1922 Kentucky Derby.

READ ABOUT

The Kentucky
Dam was built to
provide electricity
to rural areas.

1904

*The Black Patch War
breaks out in western
Kentucky*

1930

*Drought strikes
Kentucky*

▲**1931**

*Coal miners in
Harlan go on strike*

C H A P T E R   F I V E

MORE MODERN TIMES

★

KENTUCKY ENTERED THE 20TH CENTURY FACING BIG CHALLENGES. Its industries were growing but not as rapidly as those in other states. However, relief came through New Deal programs of the 1930s. The state weathered its problems, and its cities grew.

1945

The Kentucky Dam is completed

1966

Kentucky's legislature passes a strong civil rights law

▲2006

Toyota begins making hybrid Camrys in Georgetown

Armed guards helped protect some tobacco farmers during the Black Patch War.

THE BLACK PATCH WAR

At the start of the 20th century, tobacco companies and growers clashed over the price that companies were paying for the product. Some growers banded together, refusing to sell their tobacco until they received fair prices from the big companies. Some growers, though, didn't join the movement because they could not afford to give up the income from tobacco sales. Disagreements between growers who banded together and those who refused led to violence. In the Black Patch District of western Kentucky in 1904, raiders attacked farmers who refused to join the movement, burning warehouses and damaging crops. The conflict became known as the Black Patch War, or the Tobacco War. Violence raged for several years before state officials were able to stop it.

WINNING THE RIGHT TO VOTE

At the start of the 20th century, women in Kentucky and elsewhere in the United States could not vote in most elections. In the first decades of the new century, leaders in the movement for woman suffrage (the right to vote) sought to change that. Kentucky women had banded together to win that right as early as 1881, when they formed the first woman suffrage group in the South. By 1888, that group was called the Kentucky Equal Rights Association and was led by Laura Clay. The daughter of antislavery leader Cassius M. Clay, she became a national leader in the suffrage movement, organizing women across the country to push for their rights.

Another Kentucky suffrage leader, Madeline Breckinridge, became famous for her bold speeches supporting women's rights. She helped win the right for women to vote in school board elections in 1912. The efforts of Breckinridge, Clay, and many others paid off. In 1920, the 19th Amendment to the U.S. Constitution gave women the right to vote in all elections.

MINI-BIO

LAURA CLAY: CRUSADER FOR WOMEN'S RIGHTS

Laura Clay (1849–1941) was a national leader in the women's rights movement. She became interested in women's rights when her parents divorced and she learned that women like her mother had few legal rights. She became the head of the Kentucky Equal Rights Association in 1888 and campaigned around the country to urge women to fight for their rights. Her work increased membership in the National American Woman Suffrage Association—from 17,000 in 1905 to more than 45,000 in 1907—and helped pave the way to full voting rights for women.

? Want to know more? See www.womeninkentucky.com/site/reform/l_clay.html

Coal miners pose for a photograph at the mouth of a coal mine at Elkatawa in 1890.

COAL MINING

The first commercial coal mine in Kentucky had opened in 1820 in Muhlenberg County. After the Civil War, the state's railroads carried coal from Kentucky to the nation's biggest cities, where it fueled factories. Companies were soon mining and shipping huge loads of coal out of Kentucky. As Kentucky entered the 1900s, its coal was helping to drive the nation's growing industries.

By 1910, several companies had developed large mines employing 500 miners or more each. To attract miners, in 1911 the International Harvester Company built an entire town, including a company store, school, church, and bandstand. This town, called Benham, was just like many others founded as coal-mining company towns. Companies built entire villages to house workers and their families and to provide them with all the goods and services they needed. Life in a company town offered advantages most people had never known before. But it also made workers dependent on their employers for just about everything—and companies often charged high prices for the goods and services available in the towns. Many workers soon found themselves owing money to the company, making it impossible for them to leave the company town.

UNIONS AND MINES

Coal miners spent long hours in dark, cramped underground tunnels, where explosions, accidents, or cave-ins were ever-present dangers. Many became sick from years and years of breathing coal dust.

To demand better working and living conditions and higher pay, miners formed **labor unions**. Mining companies, which didn't want to give workers a say in how their businesses were run, usually resisted the unions. Sometimes conflicts between union workers and company security forces turned violent. In 1931, unions and coal-mine operators fought battles in eastern Kentucky's Harlan County, earning the county the nickname Bloody Harlan.

WORD TO KNOW

labor unions *organizations of workers formed to protect the rights of their members, including, especially, better pay and working conditions*

Miners' wives marched in Harlan to protest the conditions in the mines.

MARY BRECKINRIDGE: CARING FOR MOTHERS AND CHILDREN

Mary Breckinridge (1881–1964) was a leader in providing nursing care to rural areas. After both of her children died very young, Breckinridge decided to devote herself to caring for mothers and children. She studied nursing and launched the Frontier Nursing Service in 1925. Its mission was to provide care to women and children in remote areas of eastern Kentucky. Nurses would travel many miles over dangerous roads to help people in need. Today, the Frontier Nursing School of Midwifery still operates from Leslie County.

? Want to know more? See www.frontiernursing. org/History/MaryBreckinridge.shtm

HARD TIMES

In the first decades of the 20th century, Kentucky farmers had to contend with competition from the booming corn and wheat belt of the midwestern states. The market for crops was changing, too. For example, hemp had been a major crop for Kentucky farmers in the 1800s, but by the 20th century, demand for hemp fell sharply as wire and iron bands replaced hemp rope.

A drought in 1930 also devastated Kentucky farmers. Some places in Kentucky went without rain for a month and a half. Crops withered. Even Kentucky's bluegrass turned brown. To make matters worse, the entire United States was mired in the Great Depression, which began after the stock market crash of 1929. Many working people found themselves jobless, without money, and unable to pay for basic family needs.

Kentuckians found some relief in federal programs called the New Deal, which were designed to ease the Depression. The Civilian Conservation Corps put 80,000 young Kentuckians to work. Among other things, they built the cabins and lodges that still stand in some Kentucky parks and forests. The Tennessee Valley Authority and the Rural Electric Administration dammed rivers and turned the rushing waters into affordable electricity. The mammoth Kentucky Dam was completed in 1945. It helped bring electricity to sections of rural Kentucky that had never had access to it.

When the United States entered World War II in 1941, the massive industrial effort that followed had a dramatic impact on Kentucky. The demand for equipment and supplies for the armed forces provided a boost to Kentucky's economy—and to the nation's. One Ford Motor Company factory in Louisville produced some 100,000 jeeps. This and other factories and mines in Kentucky helped fuel the U.S. military.

Some 300,000 Kentuckians served in the armed forces. Seven Kentuckians earned Congressional Medals of Honor, the nation's highest award for bravery. Thousands of U.S. troops trained at Kentucky's Fort Knox and Camp Breckinridge.

CIVIL RIGHTS

The 20th century also marked a long struggle for African American civil rights. In Kentucky, as in other southern states at the start of the century, **segregation** was a fact of life. African Americans attended separate schools and had to use separate public facilities. The Day Law, enacted in 1904, made it illegal for blacks and whites to be educated together.

African Americans in Kentucky cities worked to end segregation. They organized **sit-ins** and other protests. In 1954, the U.S. Supreme Court ruled that segregation in public education was illegal. Schools would have to open their doors to all races. While other southern states defied the federal government's orders, Kentucky moved ahead to end school segregation.

WORDS TO KNOW

segregation *separation from others, according to race, class, ethnic group, religion, or other factors*

sit-ins *acts of protest that involve sitting in racially segregated places and refusing to leave*

MINI-BIO

SUZY POST: FREEDOM FIGHTER

While Kentucky had some of the first schools in the nation to integrate, not all schools there did so. In 1975, Suzy Post, mother of five, brought a lawsuit to desegregate classes in Louisville. White and black parents and children cooperated in a school desegregation plan. In 2007, she spoke of its success: "Make no mistake: Black, white, Latino, and Asians interacting on a daily basis has a profound relationship to the vitality of our community and to positive community growth."

? **Want to know more?** See http://kchr.ky.gov/hof/halloffame2007.htm?&pageOrder=1&selectedPic=10

Civil rights protesters in Louisville blocked the path of a police car after others in their group had been arrested in 1964.

MINI-BIO

WHITNEY M. YOUNG JR.: CIVIL RIGHTS LEADER

Born in Shelby County, Whitney M. Young Jr. (1921–1971) became a national leader in the civil rights movement in the 1960s. A graduate of Kentucky State College (now Kentucky State University), he became director of the National Urban League, a civil rights organization, in 1961. He used his prominence in the civil rights movement to call attention to the problem of poverty among African Americans. He worked to attack the root causes of poverty, including poor health, inadequate housing, and the lack of educational opportunities.

? **Want to know more?** See www.medaloffreedom. com/WhitneyYoung.htm

In 1966, Kentucky passed a civil rights law that prohibited racial discrimination in workplaces and guaranteed "full and equal" access to public services. Civil rights leader Martin Luther King Jr. called it "the strongest and most comprehensive civil rights bill passed by a southern state." Much more still needed to be done to achieve full equality for African Americans. But by desegregating its public schools and passing a strong civil rights law, Kentucky took a leadership role in the struggle for civil rights.

Strip mining often removes entire mountaintops to get to coal deposits.

ENVIRONMENT

Industries such as coal mining and logging have played an important part in Kentucky's growth, but they have also contributed to environmental problems. At the start of the 20th century, logging was one of Kentucky's biggest industries, employing 30,000 people. But often loggers gave little thought to preserving or replacing the forests they cut down. As early as 1905, state officials worried that Kentucky's forests were being destroyed "without regard for the future." Today, managing the state's forest resources is increasingly important for Kentuckians. Over the last several decades, Kentucky has organized efforts to preserve its forests, including more effective fire prevention and response programs. The state's Division of Forestry maintains nurseries and educates landowners about the importance of managing the state's forest resources.

Coal mining's impact on the environment was dramatic, too. Beginning around 1940, more and more miners practiced surface mining, or strip mining, to remove coal. Less costly than underground mining, surface mining peels away the top layers of earth to

THINK ABOUT IT!

Tougher Rules for Coal Mining?

The most effective and least expensive way to mine coal is called surface mining—peeling away top layers of soil and rocks on mountainsides to get at the coal beneath. The leftover rock and dirt is dumped into valleys, where it sometimes buries or pollutes small streams.

Coal-mining companies have resisted some efforts to pass government rules that would protect the environment from the effects of surface mining. They point out that coal mining is already tightly regulated. Bill Caylor of the Kentucky Coal Association told *The Courier-Journal,* a Louisville newspaper, that coal mining has only a "temporary impact" on rivers and streams. Mining supporters add that coal mining brings jobs and money to Kentucky; creating tougher rules would only make mining more expensive and hurt Kentucky's economy. As Tom Lewis, who worked in the Kentucky coal industry for years, said, coal mining has given "great jobs" to residents and "raised the standard of living in the area."

Opponents of surface mining say that it destroys mountains and pollutes rivers. They would like to see new, tougher rules in place to stop the practice or make it less destructive. Some urge coal companies to find less harmful ways to dispose of leftover soil. "Coal companies have a right to their coal," said the Rev. John Rausch, a Catholic priest opposed to surface mining. "They also have a responsibility to mine it in a responsible way." He says that mining practices that damage the environment represent "a disregard for the common good."

Sources: *The Courier-Journal* of Louisville, December 31, 2006, and *The Anniston Star* of Anniston, Alabama, September 16, 2007

get at coal deposits that lie below. The process left ugly gashes in Kentucky's landscape and destroyed whole hillsides. It also eroded soil so badly that it easily washed away in storms and polluted local water supplies. By 1974, more than half of Kentucky's coal production came from surface mining.

Concern about surface mining's environmental impact resulted in changes to Kentucky's laws governing coal mining. In 1966, Kentucky's legislature adopted a new mining law, restricting the amount of soil that could be stripped away. The Federal Surface Mining Control and Reclamation Act of 1977 placed even more restrictions on surface mining.

THE 21ST CENTURY

Two tragic accidents struck Kentucky in 2006. In May, an underground explosion in a Harlan County coal mine killed five men. The accident called attention to the need to ensure worker safety in Kentucky's mines. Then in August, a plane crash killed 49 of the 50 people aboard a flight leaving Lexington's Blue Grass Airport.

As they moved into a new century, Kentuckians continued to try to make their state an attractive place to work, live, and raise families. Campaigns to draw major employers to Kentucky scored big victories. In 2005, the auto company Toyota announced that it would build the Camry, its hybrid car, at its Georgetown plant. In 2006, the first Camrys rolled out. The package delivery company UPS in 2006 announced a $1 billion project to expand its facility in Louisville. These projects promise to bring thousands of new jobs to Kentucky.

Building a Toyota in Georgetown

68

READ ABOUT

A crowd takes
in the fun at
the Kentucky
State Fair.

CHAPTER SIX

PEOPLE

★

NEIGHBORS CHEER ON THEIR LOCAL HIGH SCHOOL BASKET-BALL TEAM IN A CROWDED GYM. Workers start their shift at the auto factory. Families hike and fish in a scenic state park. Kids on a field trip visit a horse farm to learn about caring for animals. More than a million people hit the streets of Louisville for the fireworks and fun of the Kentucky Derby Festival. These are just a few of the ways Kentuckians celebrate, learn, play, and live in their state.

In the summer, children play in the fountains in downtown Louisville.

In Kentucky, about 106 people live in a typical square mile (41 per sq km), placing it 23rd among U.S. states in population density rankings.

CITY AND COUNTRY

Slightly more than half of Kentuckians live in cities. That's a dramatic change from the past. Even as late as the 1960s, most Kentuckians lived in rural areas. But since then, the cities and suburbs of Kentucky have grown rapidly.

Today, most of Kentucky's population lives in an area bounded by Louisville, Lexington, and the northern Kentucky communities of Covington and Newport. This area is sometimes called the Golden Triangle, and it has a combined population of about 2.5 million.

While Kentucky's cities and suburbs have grown, many rural counties have seen their populations decrease. For example, the population of Harlan County in eastern Kentucky fell by more than 3,000 people—a 9.2 percent drop—from 1990 to 2000. Why do people leave rural areas for cities and suburbs? Often, they are seeking better jobs, schools, and other opportunities to improve their quality of life.

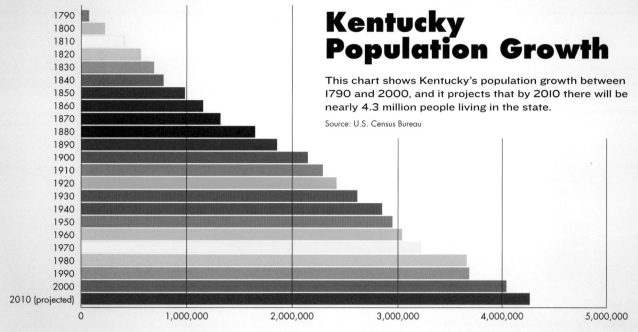

Kentucky Population Growth

This chart shows Kentucky's population growth between 1790 and 2000, and it projects that by 2010 there will be nearly 4.3 million people living in the state.

Source: U.S. Census Bureau

A KENTUCKY MIX

About nine in ten Kentuckians identify themselves as white. Of those white Kentuckians, most claim English, Scottish, or German backgrounds. African Americans make up about 7.5 percent of Kentucky's population, and they are concentrated in the commonwealth's biggest cities. Hispanic, or Latino, people make up a fast-growing part of Kentucky's population. Between 1990 and 2000, the Hispanic population doubled. Today, more than 80,000 Hispanic people live in Kentucky's cities and its rural countryside. According to one estimate, by 2018, about 8 percent of Kentucky high school graduates will be Hispanic.

People QuickFacts

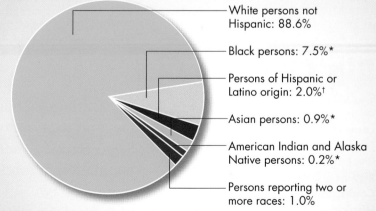

White persons not Hispanic: 88.6%

Black persons: 7.5%*

Persons of Hispanic or Latino origin: 2.0%†

Asian persons: 0.9%*

American Indian and Alaska Native persons: 0.2%*

Persons reporting two or more races: 1.0%

*Hispanics may be of any race, so they also are included in applicable race categories
†Includes persons reporting only one race
Source: U.S. Census Bureau, 2005 estimate

Where Kentuckians Live

The colors on this map indicate population density throughout the state. The darker the color, the more people live there.

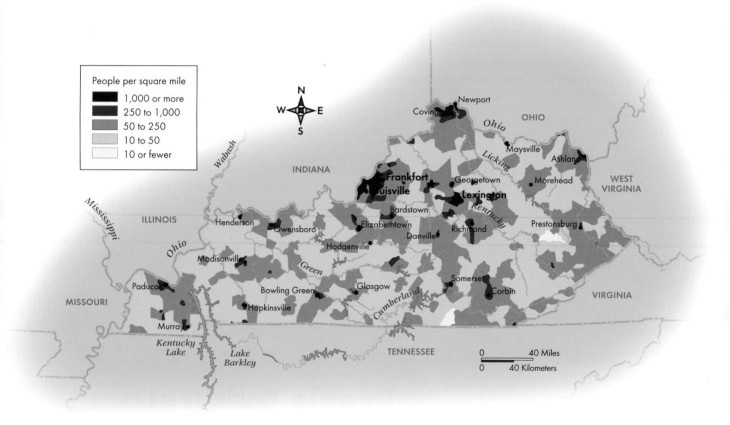

People per square mile
- 1,000 or more
- 250 to 1,000
- 50 to 250
- 10 to 50
- 10 or fewer

Big City Life

This list shows the population of Kentucky's biggest cities.

Louisville	554,496
Lexington-Fayette	270,789
Owensboro	55,525
Bowling Green	53,176
Covington	42,797
Hopkinsville	27,415
Paducah	25,661

Source: U.S. Census Bureau, 2006 estimates

Kentucky's Asian American population is growing, too, and today it totals about 38,000 people. More than 8,000 Native Americans live in Kentucky. Kentucky's population of foreign-born people is small. Just a little more than two out of every 100 Kentuckians were born outside of the United States.

EDUCATION

Kentucky created its first public school system in 1838 and for many years struggled to provide a quality education to all students. By the end of the 1900s, Kentucky students scored below national averages on standardized tests. The state also had one of the lowest high school graduation rates in the country—one in three adult Kentuckians had not graduated from high school as of 1990.

Governor Martha Layne Collins, a former teacher, asked the state's legislature to provide increased funding for schools in the mid-1980s. But Kentucky courts demanded more sweeping changes in education. In 1988, courts ruled that state money for schools was

Kentucky has made improvements in its education system to ensure that teachers are able to give adequate attention to students.

MINI-BIO

MARY LEVI SMITH: PIONEERING EDUCATOR

Mary Levi Smith (1936—), a professor of education, became the president of Kentucky State University in 1991. That made her the first African American woman to head a college in Kentucky. Smith grew up in a poor household in Mississippi. Inspired by her parents' commitment to education, she decided to become a teacher, and she later taught in public schools in Kentucky, Mississippi, and Tennessee. She once said that the purpose of education is "to prepare students for life, which means preparing them for learning throughout their lifetimes."

? **Want to know more?** See www.uky.edu/Education/hofamers/smith.html

Q8 WHAT IS KENTUCKY'S OLDEST COLLEGE?

A8 The history of colleges and universities in Kentucky dates back to 1780, when Transylvania University was founded. Not only was Transylvania University Kentucky's first college, it was the first founded west of the Allegheny Mountains and the 16th in the United States. Today, it is a nationally ranked liberal arts college.

not distributed fairly: schools in some wealthy areas received more funding than schools in poor areas. And a 1989 court decision ruled that the entire educational system violated the state's constitution because that funding practice was unfair.

In response, Kentucky's legislature made changes to the public education system, passing the Kentucky Education Reform Act of 1990. It gave local school councils greater control over how they would educate their students. This was an important change for many people because they believed that local school councils would best understand the needs of the children in each community. The act also increased funding for schools, resulting in more classrooms and smaller class sizes. By 2004, Kentucky ranked 15th among the 50 states in the number of teachers provided for each student. That means students in Kentucky benefited from more personal attention from teachers than students in 35 other states.

Some 664,606 students attended Kentucky public schools in 2006. Thousands of other students attended private schools or were educated at home.

The state receives high marks for providing access to educational technology for students. A national education magazine ranked Kentucky seventh among the

University of Louisville football players greet their fans after a game.

50 states in using technology in schools and praised the quality of teaching in Kentucky schools. And over the last decade, Kentucky students' test scores in math and reading have improved. Today, the state's fourth- and eighth-graders are ahead of national scores in reading.

Kentucky is home to more than 70 colleges and universities. Two of the best known are the University of Louisville, which traces its history back to 1837, and the University of Kentucky, founded in 1865.

The University of Louisville's hospital was the birthplace of the modern civilian ambulance.

Smoking grills at a Kentucky barbeque

HOW TO TALK LIKE A KENTUCKIAN

Planning a visit to Kentucky and want to sound like a native Kentuckian? One of the most exciting times to visit is the first Saturday in May, when the annual Kentucky Derby is run in Louisville, which most Kentuckians pronounce "Lou-uh-vul." The race is held at Churchill Downs, but some natives just call it "the Downs." Look for the "twin spires"—the two towers atop the Churchill Downs grandstand are a famous landmark. But if you can't make it to the race, just read about it in the "C-J." That's the *Courier-Journal*, a daily newspaper in Louisville.

HOW TO EAT LIKE A KENTUCKIAN

Thanks to the KFC fast-food chain, Kentucky fried chicken is famous the world over. But there's much more to Kentucky cooking. From barbecue to burgoo to biscuits, there's something for every taste. So dig in!

MENU

WHAT'S ON THE MENU IN KENTUCKY?

★ ★ ★

Burgoo

This is a traditional Kentucky stew made with meat and vegetables. This stew was often made for community gatherings. Everyone would contribute something for the stew, such as meat or vegetables, which went into a large pot. Because of the pot's large size, long pieces of wood were used to stir the stew.

Hot Brown

Named for Louisville's Brown Hotel, this is an open-faced sandwich with turkey, bacon, and tomatoes.

Fried Chicken

Try some at the Sanders Café and Museum in Corbin. It was built in the 1930s by Colonel Harland Sanders and grew into the KFC fast-food chain.

Hoppin' John

Tradition says to eat this dish of black-eyed peas and rice on New Year's Day, for good luck.

Chocolate nut pie— topped with ice cream

TRY THIS RECIPE
Chocolate Nut Pie

This is a "must" at any Kentucky Derby party. Just be sure to have a grown-up nearby to help.

Ingredients:
½ cup margarine, melted
1 cup sugar
½ cup flour
2 eggs, lightly beaten
1 teaspoon vanilla
¾ cup chopped pecans or walnuts
¾ cup chocolate chips
1 9-inch pie crust, unbaked

Instructions:
1. Preheat the oven to 350 degrees.
2. Mix the ingredients in the order given.
3. Pour into the unbaked pie crust.
4. Bake for 30 minutes, or until the middle is set.

Source: Office of Senator Mitch McConnell

Fried chicken

Hoppin' John

BILL MONROE: FATHER OF BLUEGRASS MUSIC

Bill Monroe (1911–1996) was born in Rosine. He was still a teenager when he began performing on national radio shows in the 1930s. In 1938, he formed a band called the Blue Grass Boys, named for his native state. People started calling Monroe's style of music "bluegrass," and he helped make blue-grass music famous around the world. Monroe has been honored by both the Country Music Hall of Fame and the Rock and Roll Hall of Fame.

? Want to know more? See http://www.rockhall.com/inductee/bill-monroe

KENTUCKY MUSIC

"Plain music that tells a story." That's how Kentucky-born singer and mandolin player Bill Monroe once described the style of music known as bluegrass. And no one knew more about bluegrass than Monroe, who is considered the Father of Bluegrass. Based on old-time mountain music played on stringed instruments, bluegrass is just one of the styles of music that Kentuckians have embraced. From country to jazz to pop, Kentucky musicians have made their mark in a big way.

A group of musicians perform at the Festival of the Bluegrass at the Kentucky Horse Park.

Country music stars Loretta Lynn, Naomi and Wynonna Judd, Dwight Yoakam, and Ricky Skaggs all hail from the Bluegrass State. So did jazz great Lionel Hampton and singer Rosemary Clooney.

ARTISTS, AUTHORS, AND ACTORS

One of the first Kentucky artists to win great fame was John James Audubon. Born in what is now Haiti, Audubon moved in 1808 to Louisville, where he opened a general store. Soon he began roaming the Kentucky woodlands and painting the birds and wildlife he saw. He had a remarkable talent for creating lifelike portraits of birds. Between 1827 and 1838, Audubon published collections of prints called *The Birds of America*. He is still regarded worldwide as one of the greatest nature artists. His work can be seen at the John James Audubon State Park and Museum in Henderson.

The first Kentucky author to win national acclaim was James Lane Allen (1849–1925), who wrote novels set amid the estates of the Bluegrass region. Robert Penn Warren (1905–1989) was probably the most distinguished of Kentucky's

LORETTA LYNN: COAL MINER'S DAUGHTER AND COUNTRY SUPERSTAR

Loretta Lynn (1935–) was born in a one-room log cabin in Butcher Hollow, where her father worked as a coal miner, and she became one of country music's greatest stars. Growing up, she loved listening to and singing along with country music. She soon began writing and performing her own songs. Beginning in 1960, she recorded and released a string of more than 22 top-10 hits. Her autobiography, *Coal Miner's Daughter*, was made into a movie. She was inducted into the Country Music Hall of Fame in 1988.

Want to know more? See www.lorettalynn.com/bio/

Kentucky Warbler by John James Audubon

Quilts on display at the Museum of the American Quilter's Society

authors. He was named poet laureate of the United States in 1986 and is the only writer to have won Pulitzer Prizes in both fiction and poetry. Rebecca Caudill (1899–1985) wrote popular books for young readers. Her *Tree of Freedom* won a prestigious Newbery Honor in 1949. A well-known contemporary Kentucky writer is Wendell Berry (1934–). His poems, essays, and novels, such as *The Memory of Old Jack*, express a farmer's love for the land. The stories of Bobbie Ann Mason (1940–) feature small-town life and have received much praise.

Crafts have always been an important part of life in Kentucky. In its early frontier days, settlers made baskets, pottery, quilts, and furniture. People with a special talent for such crafts were highly regarded. Kentuckians still celebrate folk arts and crafts today and honor artists such as the self-taught wood sculptor Minnie Adkins. Crafts shops and folk art galleries and museums help preserve traditions passed down from frontier days, displaying everything from traditional musical instruments to handmade toys. Berea is the official Folk Arts and Crafts Capital of Kentucky and is home to the Kentucky Artisans Center, which displays work produced by Kentucky artists. Paducah is home to the Museum of the American Quilter's Society, which displays quilts made by contemporary artists.

Kentucky is known for the dramatic arts, too. The Actors Theatre of Louisville was founded in 1963 and quickly earned a reputation as one of the best regional theaters in the nation. Louisville's Humana Festival of New American Plays has helped produce important new work by American playwrights. Frankfort-born director George C. Wolfe began life attending segregated schools and grew up to win two Tony Awards. And Kentucky has produced famous actors such as George Clooney, Johnny Depp, Ashley Judd, and Tom Cruise.

MINI-BIO

JOHNNY DEPP: SCREEN STAR

Captain Jack Sparrow may be a pirate of the Caribbean, but his roots are in Kentucky. Johnny Depp (1963–), the actor who plays the fictional Sparrow in the blockbuster Pirates of the Caribbean movies, was born in Owensboro. Depp first won fame on the 1980s TV show 21 Jump Street, but his career soon expanded to include films such as Edward Scissorhands and Charlie and the Chocolate Factory.

? Want to know more? See http://www.imdb.com/name/nm0000136/bio

SPORTS

In Kentucky, basketball isn't just a sport, it's a passion. Whether it's a high school game or a college championship, Kentuckians love to cheer on their favorite teams. And they've had a lot to cheer about over the years. The University of Kentucky has won seven NCAA basketball championships, and no other college team has won more games than the Wildcats. The University of Louisville has a proud basketball tradition of its own, including two national championships. Since 1920, the state high school basketball tournament has been one of the most popular sporting events in Kentucky.

MUHAMMAD ALI: THE GREATEST

Born Cassius Clay (1942–) in Louisville, Muhammad Ali is perhaps the greatest heavyweight boxer of all time. Ali won his first championship in 1964, but his title was taken away in 1967 when he refused to serve in the military during the Vietnam War. Forbidden to fight professionally, he toured the United States speaking about civil rights. He returned to boxing in 1970 and went on to win two more titles, which no one had ever done before. He has led campaigns to help poor children all over the globe and was awarded a Presidential Medal of Freedom.

? Want to know more? See www.ali.com/greatest/

The University of Kentucky women's basketball team plays a game against the University of Georgia at Rupp Arena in Lexington.

One of the biggest recent changes in the sports world in Kentucky and elsewhere has been expanded opportunities for girls and young women. This is because of the 1972 law called Title IX. Title IX declares that no student should be denied the benefits of any educational program or activity based on gender. Before Title IX became law, many schools offered more varsity sports teams and other activities for boys than for girls. Today, Title IX experts say that Kentucky is one of the nation's leaders in ensuring that girls and boys enjoy equal opportunities on the playing field.

Horse racing has been part of life in Kentucky since before statehood. The main horse-racing event is the Kentucky Derby, which attracts about 155,000 fans each May and turns Louisville into one big party. The race is held at Churchill Downs, the track that locals know affectionately as "the Downs." As the first jewel in the Triple Crown of U.S. Thoroughbred Racing, the Kentucky Derby is the most important horse race in the United States.

MAN O' WAR

Man O' War may have been the greatest racehorse ever. In 1919 and 1920, he entered 21 races and won 20 of them, setting five world records along the way. After he died in 1947, nearly 1,000 people attended the burial ceremony. A monument in Lexington marks his grave. One of his offspring, War Admiral, won the Kentucky Derby in 1937.

The 132nd Kentucky Derby at Churchill Downs in Louisville in 2006

WOW

The Kentucky Derby is the oldest organized sporting event of any kind in the South and the second-oldest in the entire United States.

READ ABOUT

Students on a field trip visit the Old State Capitol in Frankfort.

CHAPTER SEVEN

GOVERNMENT

★

KENTUCKY IS ONE OF JUST FOUR STATES IN THE COUNTRY THAT OFFICIALLY CALLS ITSELF A COMMONWEALTH, A STATE BASED ON LAWS THAT SERVE THE COMMON "WEAL," OR THE COMMON GOOD. Why does Kentucky call itself a commonwealth? It followed Virginia's example. Before Kentucky became a state, it was part of Virginia. In 1785, Kentuckians asked that Kentucky be made "a free and independent state to be known by the name of the 'commonwealth' of Kentucky." In the United States, commonwealths function just like other states in the Union.

Capitol Facts

Here are some fascinating facts about Kentucky's state capitol.

Dates of construction 1905–1909
Cost of construction . . . .$1.8 million
Location . . . . .700 Capitol Avenue, Frankfort
Height of Abraham Lincoln statue . . . . . .14 feet (4.3 m)
Columns in the center of the capitol . . .36, each 26 feet
(8 m) tall and weighing 10 tons

WORD TO KNOW

renovated *cleaned, improved, or rebuilt*

The current capitol is listed on the U.S. National Register of Historic Places.

KENTUCKY'S STATE CAPITOLS

In 1792, in a log cabin in Lexington, lawmakers voted to make Frankfort Kentucky's permanent capital. Today's capitol is much grander than that first log cabin. Construction on the current building began in 1905, and it opened in time for the 1910 session of the General Assembly. The dome is modeled after the one over the French emperor Napoleon's tomb in Paris. The staircases are modeled after the Grand Opera House in Paris. The capitol was **renovated** in 1955 and again in 1996.

Capital City

This map shows places of interest in Frankfort, Kentucky's capital city.

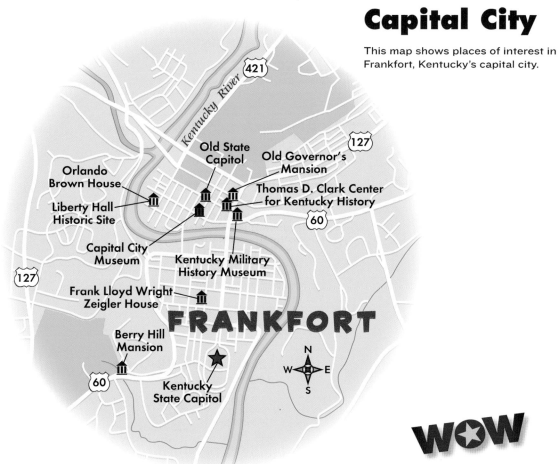

KENTUCKY'S STATE GOVERNMENT

When people in a state think that their constitution needs changes or updating, they can vote to create a new one. Kentucky has had four constitutions since its founders drafted the first one in 1792 in their bid for statehood. Its current constitution was written in 1891.

Kentucky's constitution divides the commonwealth's government into three branches: the legislative, executive, and judicial.

WOW

On the grounds of the state capitol, you can check the time on a huge clock face made of more than 10,000 flowers.

IT'S THE LAW!

A duel is an arranged fight with weapons between two people. During the early years of Kentucky statehood, a duel was considered an honorable way to settle a dispute. But so many people lost their lives in duels that Kentucky passed an anti-dueling law in 1849. To this day, it is illegal for people who have fought duels to hold public office.

Kentucky State Government

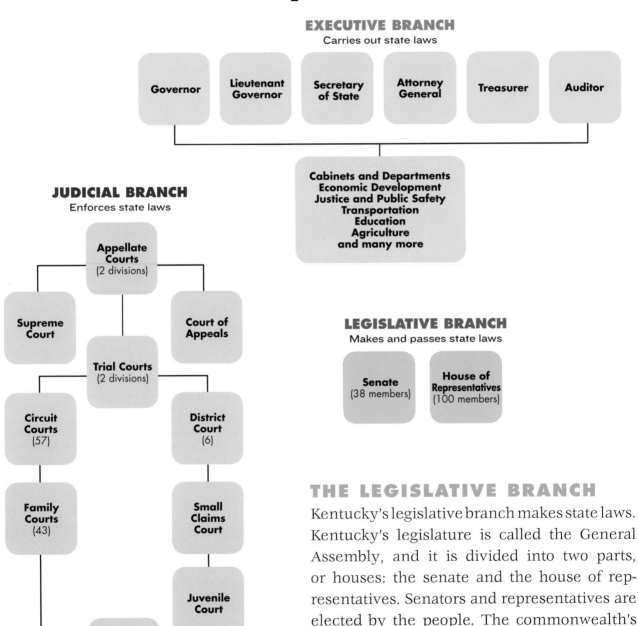

EXECUTIVE BRANCH
Carries out state laws

Governor

Lieutenant Governor

Secretary of State

Attorney General

Treasurer

Auditor

Cabinets and Departments
Economic Development
Justice and Public Safety
Transportation
Education
Agriculture
and many more

JUDICIAL BRANCH
Enforces state laws

Appellate Courts
(2 divisions)

Supreme Court

Court of Appeals

Trial Courts
(2 divisions)

Circuit Courts
(57)

District Court
(6)

Family Courts
(43)

Small Claims Court

Juvenile Court

Drug Court

LEGISLATIVE BRANCH
Makes and passes state laws

Senate
(38 members)

House of Representatives
(100 members)

THE LEGISLATIVE BRANCH

Kentucky's legislative branch makes state laws. Kentucky's legislature is called the General Assembly, and it is divided into two parts, or houses: the senate and the house of representatives. Senators and representatives are elected by the people. The commonwealth's 38 state senators serve four-year terms in office; 100 representatives serve two-year terms. Kentuckians also elect lawmakers to represent Kentucky in the national government in Washington, D.C. Kentucky sends six representatives to the House of Representatives and two senators to the Senate.

EXECUTIVE BRANCH

The job of Kentucky's executive branch is to enforce laws. The head of the executive branch is the governor, who is elected by the people of Kentucky every four years. The governor's office is in the state capitol in Frankfort. Other elected officials serving in the executive branch include the lieutenant governor, secretary of state, and attorney general. They all help keep the government running smoothly. The governor also oversees agencies or departments related to different aspects of life in Kentucky. For example, Kentucky's education cabinet promotes learning for both children and adults.

THE JUDICIAL BRANCH

The judicial branch is home to Kentucky's courts. Their job is to interpret the laws passed by the legislature and enforced by the executive branch. The courts also protect the rights of Kentucky's citizens. There are four levels of

MINI-BIO

MARTHA LAYNE COLLINS: TEACHER/GOVERNOR

Martha Layne Collins (1936—) was the first woman to become governor of Kentucky. Before running for office, she taught in Louisville-area high schools. She ran for and was elected lieutenant governor in 1979 and was elected governor in 1983. She worked to improve Kentucky schools and bring new industries to the state. One of her biggest accomplishments was convincing the car company Toyota to build a factory near Georgetown, which opened in 1988. It produced thousands of new jobs for Kentuckians. Collins is currently a scholar in residence at Georgetown College.

? Want to know more? See www. womeninkentucky.com/site/public_service/ m_collins.html

Representing Kentucky

This list shows the number of elected officials who represent Kentucky, both on the state and national levels.

OFFICE	NUMBER	LENGTH OF TERM
State senators	38	4 years
State representatives	100	2 years
U.S. senators	2	6 years
U.S. representatives	6	2 years
Presidential electors	8	—

courts in Kentucky. District courts settle most of the state's legal matters, including criminal cases and civil cases. Circuit courts hear cases involving more serious crimes. The court of appeals reviews decisions of the lower courts. And the supreme court is the final word on legal matters in Kentucky.

Kentucky Counties

This map shows the 120 counties in Kentucky. Frankfort, the state capital, is indicated with a star.

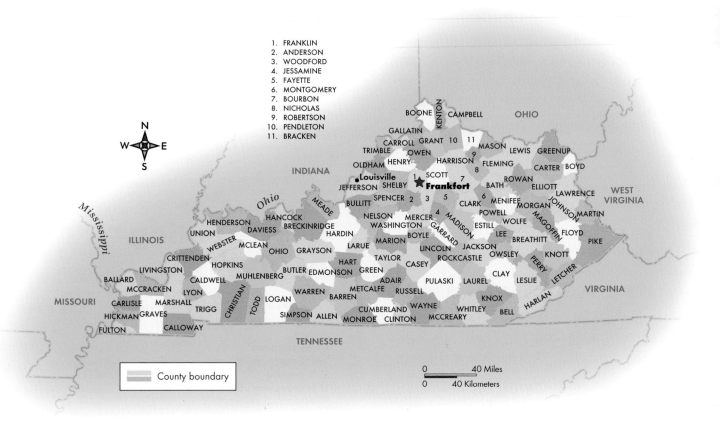

1. FRANKLIN
2. ANDERSON
3. WOODFORD
4. JESSAMINE
5. FAYETTE
6. MONTGOMERY
7. BOURBON
8. NICHOLAS
9. ROBERTSON
10. PENDLETON
11. BRACKEN

County boundary

0   40 Miles
0   40 Kilometers

In 2006, the General Assembly discussed recent changes to state tax laws.

MINI-BIO

ALBERT BENJAMIN "HAPPY" CHANDLER: POLITICAL GIANT

Born in Corydon, Albert Benjamin "Happy" Chandler (1898–1991) was governor from 1935 to 1939 and from 1955 to 1959, and also served as a U.S. senator from 1939 to 1945. He was commissioner of Major League Baseball (1945–1951), overseeing the racial integration of the league in 1947, when Jackie Robinson, an African American, began playing for the Brooklyn Dodgers. In 1956, as governor, Chandler enforced a federal court order to integrate Kentucky schools.

❓ **Want to know more?** See http://mlb.mlb.com/mlb/history/mlb_history_people.jsp?story=com_bio_2

LOCAL GOVERNMENTS

Along with its state government, Kentucky also has local and county governments. In fact, Kentucky has 120 counties—more than any other state except Texas and Georgia. A county judge-executive leads each county government, which is governed by a county fiscal court. The voters of each county elect the members of the court. County governments provide services such as taking care of roads, and they also help provide money for schools.

There are more than 400 **municipalities** in Kentucky. The Kentucky legislature divides them into six categories based on their population. The largest of these cities are called first-class cities, and the smallest are called sixth-class cities.

WORD TO KNOW

municipalities *self-governing cities or towns*

KENTUCKIANS IN THE WHITE HOUSE

Kentucky has produced two U.S. presidents—one was born in Kentucky, and the other was raised in the state.

Abraham Lincoln (1809–1865), the 16th president of the United States, was born near Hodgenville. He served as president from 1861 to 1865 and led the United States through the Civil War. Most historians rank him as one of the greatest presidents.

Zachary Taylor (1784–1850), the 12th president of the United States, was born in Virginia but moved to Kentucky with his family when he was a boy. He was raised on the family's plantation in Jefferson County. Before he became president, he served as a general in the Mexican War (1846–1848).

MINI-BIO

ABRAHAM LINCOLN: KENTUCKY-BORN PRESIDENT

Abraham Lincoln (1809–1865) once wrote that his earliest recollection was of his childhood home near Hodgenville, where he spent the first seven years of his life. Then in 1816, he moved to Indiana with the rest of his family. After he settled in Springfield, Illinois, as a young lawyer, he became active in politics. He served in the U.S. House of Representatives from 1847 to 1849. In 1858, he ran for the U.S. Senate but lost the election to Stephen A. Douglas. In 1860, Lincoln ran for and was elected president. As president, he led the country through the Civil War but did not survive to reunite it. He was killed by an assassin's bullet on April 15, 1865.

? Want to know more? See www.whitehouse.gov/history/presidents/al16.html

ON THE NATIONAL LEVEL

In addition to two U.S. presidents, Kentuckians have served in other important positions in the federal government.

Frederick Moore Vinson (1890–1953) was chief justice of the United States from 1946 to 1953. Before that, he represented Kentucky in the U.S. Congress.

John Marshall Harlan (1833–1911) was a Union colonel in the Civil War before entering Kentucky politics. Appointed to the Supreme Court, he expressed fiercely independent views. When the other justices voted to approve racial segregation, he alone disagreed. He said that segregation pinned the "badge of inferiority" on people of color and was "a thin disguise" for discrimination that perpetuated forms of slavery. "The destinies of the two races, in this country, are indissolubly linked together," he said, "and the interest of both require that the common government of all shall not permit seeds of race hate to be planted under the sanction of law."

Louis Brandeis (1856–1941) was a U.S. Supreme Court justice from 1916 to 1939. He was sometimes called "the people's attorney" for his defense of individual human rights. He was the first American of Jewish ancestry to serve on the Court.

ISSUES FOR THE FUTURE

Kentucky has always called itself a commonwealth, and serving the common good remains the main challenge of the state government. Doing so will mean taking on some important issues. Providing quality public education remains a concern for many residents, as does protecting Kentucky's natural resources. Creating new jobs and attracting businesses to Kentucky is key to keeping the state thriving. The state government has an important role to play in addressing all these issues.

WOW

Inside the state capitol is a statue of native son Abraham Lincoln. According to tradition, rubbing the boots of the Lincoln statue will bring good luck.

Tulip poplar blossom

THE GREAT STATE TREE DEBATE

Kentucky's official state tree is the tulip poplar. But that fact doesn't stop some Kentuckians from arguing about what *should* be the official state tree. The debate goes back more than 30 years. In 1956, the General Assembly made the tulip poplar the state tree, but for some reason, the results of the assembly's vote were never properly recorded. The mistake was discovered in the early 1970s, and the assembly decided to take another vote in 1976. This time, they voted to make the Kentucky coffee the state tree. They chose it because it was the only tree named after the state. But supporters of the tulip poplar did not give up. They pushed for yet another vote. And in 1994, the General Assembly voted to make the tulip poplar the state tree—again.

State Flag

Kentucky's official flag has a blue field with a picture of the state seal and the words of the state motto in the middle. The state motto, "United We Stand, Divided We Fall," comes from a ballad called the "Liberty Song," which was popular during the Revolutionary War. The design of the state flag was approved by state government in 1928. The original flag is now displayed in the Kentucky History Museum in Frankfort.

State Seal

In 1792, the state legislature declared that the official seal of Kentucky must feature two friends embracing and include the state's name and motto. Since then, there have been many versions of the seal. Today, the state seal features a formally dressed man on the right, who represents England coming to Kentucky. The man in buckskin, on the left, is from the frontier. Shaking hands, they are uniting the colonial and pioneer aspects of the commonwealth. Two sprigs of goldenrod in bloom are shown in the lower portion of the seal. The official colors of the seal are blue and gold.

READ ABOUT

A huge load of coal being transported on the Ohio River

CHAPTER EIGHT

ECONOMY

★

ROM HORSES TO COAL TO BOURBON WHISKEY, KENTUCKY PRODUCTS ARE KNOWN ALL AROUND THE WORLD. But Kentucky's best-known goods make up only part of a varied and growing economy that has gone through dramatic changes in the last century. Farming and mining were once the heart of economic life in Kentucky. In recent decades, manufacturing has become big business in the commonwealth. And more and more Kentuckians make their living providing services to other people.

Two workers pick and sort the crop at a pumpkin patch in western Kentucky.

FARMING

Kentuckians remain proud of their history as a farming state. But fewer and fewer people work on Kentucky farms. Between 1975 and 1993, the number of full-time farmers in the commonwealth fell from 85,400 to 47,329. Today, only about two out of every 100 Kentuckians work solely on a farm.

Still, Kentucky farms make an impact on the life of the state and the nation. Kentucky had 84,000 farms in 2005. In 2004, Kentucky set a state record for income produced by farms: $4.13 billion. Kentucky is one of the leading tobacco-growing states in the country. It is the leading beef cattle state east of the Mississippi River. And it ranks in the top 20 in production of corn, soybeans, winter wheat, hay, barley, and sorghum.

In 2004, Kentucky was first among U.S. states in exports of livestock. Kentucky's best-known livestock export is Thoroughbred racing horses. Horses raised on Kentucky farms are sold at auctions and compete in races all around the world.

Major Agricultural and Mining Products

This map shows where Kentucky's major agricultural and mining products come from. See a cow? That means cattle is found there.

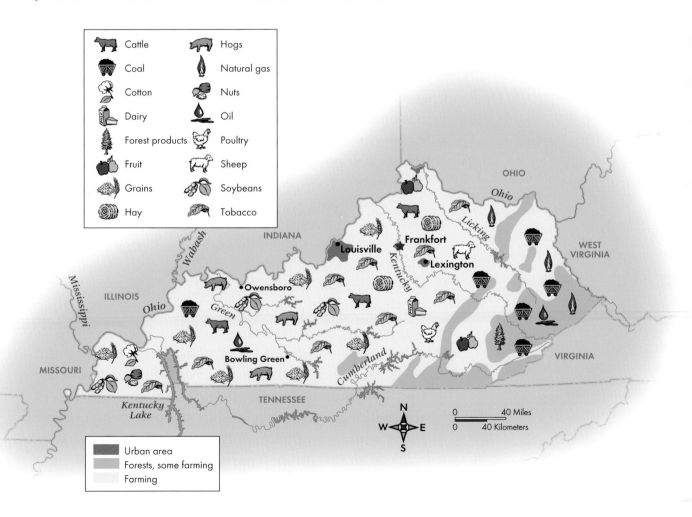

Kentucky was the nation's top coal-producing state from 1973 to 1987.

MINING

Coal mining has played a large part in Kentucky's history, as well. Coal deposits can be found under almost half of Kentucky's land. The mountains of eastern Kentucky and the Ohio River country of western Kentucky contain some of the richest coalfields in the United States.

Coal mines do not employ as many Kentuckians as they once did. By the 1960s, more mining jobs could be done more quickly and easily by machines than by humans. The number of jobs for miners in Kentucky fell rapidly in the second half of the 20th century. In 1950, Kentucky coal mines employed 66,636 people. By 1995, mining employment had fallen to 20,144. But with some 400 mines producing more than 100 million tons of coal in a year, Kentucky remains one of the nation's top three coal-producing states. Other natural resources found in Kentucky include oil, natural gas, limestone, and clay.

Kentucky's forests support another industry based on one of the state's natural resources. Logging companies began harvesting Kentucky timber in the 1800s. By 1905, Kentucky officials were warning that the state's forest resources might soon disappear. Still, loggers continued to harvest the woodlands until some counties had been so completely stripped of timber that logging stopped there. Thousands of workers lost their jobs as the logging industry in Kentucky withered. It would be decades before logging recovered in the state. By the 1990s, Kentucky ranked fourth among the states in production of hardwood lumber. In 1990, the Kentucky forest industry employed more than 24,000 workers, and its annual timber harvest was worth more than $900 million.

What Do Kentuckians Do?

This color-coded chart shows what industries Kentuckians work in.

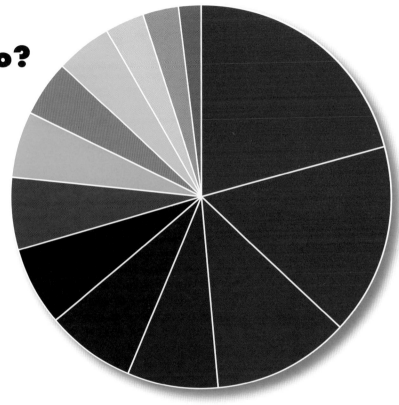

21.1% Educational services, health care, and social assistance, 383,576	**7.5%** Construction, 136,344	**4.8%** Other services, except public administration, 87,646
16.0% Manufacturing, 290,253	**6.9%** Professional, scientific, management, administrative and waste management services, 125,150	**4.7%** Public administration, 85,818
11.6% Retail trade, 211,228		**3.2%** Agriculture, forestry, fishing and hunting, and mining, 57,718
7.7% Arts, entertainment, recreation, accommodation, and food services, 138,864	**5.9%** Transportation, warehousing, and utilities, 106,763	**3.2%** Wholesale trade, 58,048
	5.6% Finance and insurance, real estate, and rental and leasing, 101,672	**1.8%** Information, 32,983

Source: U.S. Census Bureau, 2005 estimate

MANUFACTURING INDUSTRY

Kentucky sent $13 billion worth of goods to other states and countries in 2004. About $12.5 billion of those exports were manufactured goods. Kentucky ranked 19th among the 50 states in the value of its exports. In all, Kentucky's factories turn out about $50 billion worth of products each year.

There are 79,000 miles (127,000 km) of federal, state, and local roads in Kentucky. That's enough road mileage to carry you from New York to Los Angeles 28 times.

A worker at the Toyota plant in Georgetown assembles a Camry.

SEE IT HERE!

MAKING CARS

Visitors from around the world tour the Toyota factory in Georgetown. The process of making a car begins with giant rolls of steel that are cut into sheets. These eventually become part of the car's body. Parts are assembled, paint applied, and a final inspection made. In all, it takes about 20 hours for each car to go through the manufacturing process.

Automobile manufacturing is a big business in Kentucky. A Toyota factory in Georgetown produces one of the world's most popular car models, the Camry. The factory, Toyota's first in the United States and its largest in North America, is big enough to fit 156 football fields inside. And outside, there's a test track. The plant opened in 1988, creating thousands of new jobs for Kentuckians. Other popular automobiles made in Kentucky include Ford trucks and the Chevrolet Corvette. Kentucky ranks fourth among U.S. states in car and truck production. One out of every ten cars or trucks produced in the United States is made in Kentucky.

Top Products

Agriculture Tobacco, livestock, corn, soybeans
Manufacturing Cars, transportation equipment, home appliances
Natural resources Coal, limestone, clay, hardwood

Kentucky is a national leader in producing transportation equipment, including trailers and railroad cars. It leads the nation in making parts for turbojets (engines used to propel airplanes) and turbopropellers. Home appliances and electronics equipment are two other important Kentucky products.

Tourism is a vital part of Kentucky's economy. Visitors come from around the country and the world to see Kentucky's many attractions, including Mammoth Cave, the Louisville Zoo, and Cumberland Gap National Historical Park. They spend more than $5 billion in Kentucky each year. In all, about 3,500 Kentucky businesses serve visitors and tourists.

THE MILITARY

Kentucky hosts two huge U.S. Army bases. Fort Knox is home to the army's Armored Warfare Training Center, but it is best known as the place where the federal government stores its supply of gold. Fort Knox stretches over 109,000 acres (44,100 ha) near Elizabethtown. More than 10,000 military personnel work there. To the west, Fort Campbell straddles the border between Kentucky and Tennessee. The fort is home to the army's 101st Airborne Division, known as the Screaming Eagles, famed for their air assault operations.

With its natural resources and thriving factories, Kentucky's economy continues to grow. Education will play a key part in that growth. A highly educated workforce will attract businesses to Kentucky and keep the state prepared for the future.

MINI-BIO

HARLAND SANDERS: FINGER LICKIN' GOOD

Colonel Harland Sanders (1890–1980) became famous around the world for his delicious fried chicken. In the 1930s, he ran a service station in Corbin and served his home-made fried chicken to hungry travelers. His food proved to be so popular that Sanders soon opened a restaurant in Corbin. That restaurant grew into a worldwide fast-food empire known as Kentucky Fried Chicken.

 Want to know more? See www.ajskfc.com/colsanders.html

FAQ

Q8 HOW MUCH GOLD IS IN FORT KNOX?

A8 According to the U.S. Department of the Treasury, Fort Knox is home to 147.3 million ounces (4.2 million kilograms) of gold. The gold is stored in the form of solid bricks, each weighing 27.5 pounds (12.5 kg) and worth $16,888.

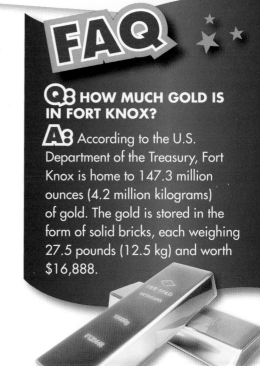

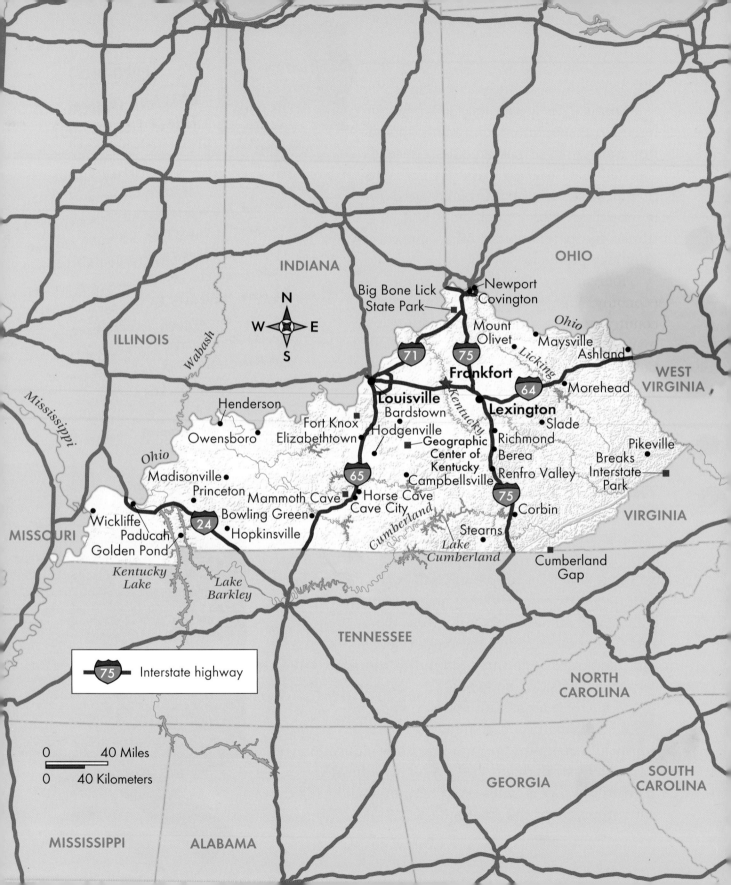

INDIANA

OHIO

ILLINOIS

N
W · E
S

Big Bone Lick
State Park

Newport
Covington

Mount
Olivet

Ohio

Maysville

Licking

Ashland

WEST
VIRGINIA

Frankfort

Louisville
Bardstown

Kentucky

64

Morehead

Henderson

Fort Knox
Hodgenville

Elizabethtown

Owensboro

Geographic
Center of
Kentucky

Campbellsville

Lexington
Richmond
Berea
Renfro Valley

Slade

Pikeville

Breaks
Interstate
Park

Mississippi

Ohio

65

Madisonville

Princeton

Mammoth Cave

Horse Cave
Cave City

Corbin

VIRGINIA

75

Wickliffe
Paducah
Golden Pond

24

Bowling Green

Hopkinsville

Cumberland

Stearns

Lake
Cumberland

Cumberland
Gap

MISSOURI

Kentucky
Lake

Lake
Barkley

TENNESSEE

NORTH
CAROLINA

75 Interstate highway

0   40 Miles

0   40 Kilometers

GEORGIA

SOUTH
CAROLINA

MISSISSIPPI   ALABAMA

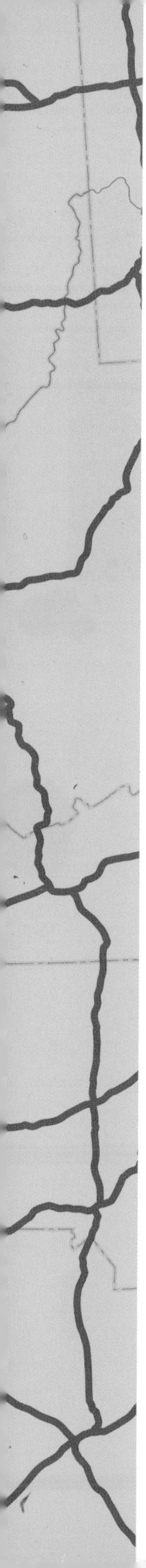

CHAPTER NINE

TRAVEL GUIDE

★

TRAVEL GUIDE

★

KENTUCKY IS A GREAT PLACE TO EXPLORE. You can take a paddle-boat ride on the Ohio River. Or see big-city bright lights and the historic streets of small towns. Hike through lush forests and over ancient mountains. Or probe some of the world's longest caves. You can even go back in time and see what life was like for pioneers. These are just a few of the experiences waiting for you in Kentucky. Let's explore!

← Follow along with this travel map. We'll begin in Cumberland Gap and travel all the way to Fort Knox.

EASTERN KENTUCKY

THINGS TO DO: Hike the Cumberland Gap, ride the Country Music Highway, and see the amazing moonbow at Cumberland Falls.

Cumberland Gap

★ **Cumberland Gap National Historical Park:** This natural break in the mountains has been a gateway to Kentucky for centuries. Today, this park features an interactive exhibit about Kentucky history and miles of hiking trails, including one route that leads to Pinnacle Overlook, 2,440 feet (744 m) above sea level.

Corbin

★ **Sanders Café and Museum:** Learn how Colonel Harland Sanders launched the business that grew into Kentucky Fried Chicken. Then order a helping of the colonel's chicken, cooked according to his original recipe.

★ **Cumberland Falls:** The second-largest waterfall east of the Rocky Mountains, these falls are called the Niagara of the South. Visit on a night with a full moon to check out the majestic moonbow that is formed by the water's mist rising in the moonlight.

Natural Bridge State Resort Park

Slade

★ **Natural Bridge State Resort Park:** The 65-foot-high (20-m) sandstone arch is one of Kentucky's natural wonders. And getting there is fun, too. Just take the Sky Lift, a ride over treetops that drops you off near the arch. You can swim, play miniature golf, or ride pedal boats.

Breaks Interstate Park

★ **The Grand Canyon of the South:** The deepest gorge east of the Mississippi River, this chasm was carved by the Russell Fork River and is 5 miles (8 km) long. Visit Powwow Cave, once a gathering place for the Shawnee; bike ride on one of the park's trails; or go horseback riding.

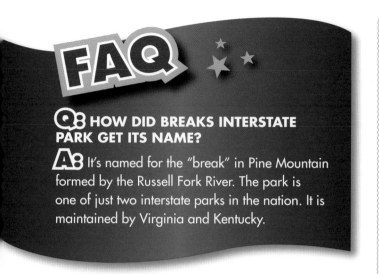

FAQ

Q8 HOW DID BREAKS INTERSTATE PARK GET ITS NAME?

A8 It's named for the "break" in Pine Mountain formed by the Russell Fork River. The park is one of just two interstate parks in the nation. It is maintained by Virginia and Kentucky.

Ashland

★ **Highlands Museum and Discovery Center:** Ever wanted a moment of music stardom? Try the Karaoke Korner stage at this fun museum, part of its salute to Kentucky's country music heritage. You can also visit an old-fashioned Ohio River landing and see what an 1870s classroom was like.

★ **Highway 23:** This road, which leads you through eastern Kentucky to the Ohio River, was declared the Country Music Highway by the Kentucky General Assembly in 1994. The highway honors the state's many country music greats, including Loretta Lynn, Crystal Gayle, and Billy Ray Cyrus, who come from points along the route.

Maysville

★ **National Underground Railroad Museum:** This museum tells the story of enslaved African Americans who tried to find a path to freedom in the North.

Morehead

★ **Kentucky Folk Art Center:** From wooden roosters to hand-carved angels, the galleries of the art center are filled with fanciful creatures. The center is devoted to traditional storytelling, dance, arts, and crafts.

Mount Olivet

★ **Blue Licks Battlefield State Park:** This was the site of a Revolutionary War battle fought in 1782, and if you visit in August, you can see a reenactment of the battle. Its Pioneer Museum features displays on Native Americans and pioneers.

Berea

★ **Kentucky Artisan Center:** Taste Kentucky specialties in the center's café, listen to music by some of the state's most talented recording artists, and check out the quilts, baskets, and pottery made by Kentucky folk artists.

Kentucky Music Hall of Fame and Museum

Renfro Valley

★ **Kentucky Music Hall of Fame and Museum:** Listen, touch, learn, and even perform at this museum honoring Kentucky's music greats. After you've taken in the exhibits about Kentucky's musical heritage, you can record your own CD!

NORTHERN KENTUCKY AND THE BLUEGRASS

THINGS TO DO: Take a steamboat ride on the Ohio River, go one-on-one with Kentucky basketball greats of the past, and get a close-up view of a shark feeding ground.

Newport

★ **World Peace Bell:** The world's largest free-swinging bell, this wonder weighs in at 66,000 pounds (30,000 kg). It's decorated with images of children holding hands beneath a starry sky. It was first rung as 1999 turned into 2000.

★ **Newport Aquarium:** Underwater tunnels and see-through floors let you get up close to the more than 7,000 aquatic creatures here. Visit an array of habitats, including an Amazon rain forest, a colorful coral reef, and a shark feeding ground.

Newport Aquarium

Covington

★ **John A. Roebling Suspension Bridge:** Named for its designer, this bridge was completed in 1866. At the time, it was the world's largest suspension bridge. It still carries thousands of cars over the Ohio River between Kentucky and Ohio each day.

Kentucky Horse Park

Kentucky's proud basketball tradition. Video and computer technology at the museum even lets you go one-on-one with great Kentucky Wildcats of the past.

Frankfort

★ **Kentucky State Capitol:** At one of the most beautiful capitols in the country, you can see where Kentucky's leaders go about the business of government. Check out the first lady doll collection, with miniatures of Kentucky's past first ladies in period dress.

SEE IT HERE!

BIG BONE LICK STATE PARK

This was one of the first places scientists from the United States encountered their nation's prehistoric past. Twelve thousand years ago, mammoths, giant bison, and other prehistoric animals came here to drink the salty water produced by springs. When they died, their bones were preserved in the boggy soil. Explorers began finding the bones in the 1700s. The bones provided important clues about the animals that once roamed Kentucky. Thomas Jefferson and Benjamin Franklin were among those who examined the fossils. Many of the bones are on display at the park's museum.

Lexington

★ **Kentucky Horse Park and The International Museum of the Horse:** The world's largest museum devoted to horses, this place is definitely hands-on. Ride a horse or pony and enjoy the daily Parade of Breeds, where you'll learn about the 24 different kinds of horses that live at the park. Then meet and pet your favorites.

★ **University of Kentucky Basketball Museum:** Kentucky is hoops heaven, and this museum is all about the University of

★ **Executive Mansion:** Across the lawn from the capitol, this impressive limestone structure has been home to Kentucky's governors since 1914 and is open to the public.

★ **Thomas D. Clark Center for Kentucky History:** This museum traces 12,000 years of Kentucky history. Don't miss the main exhibit, "Kentucky Journey." The museum's collection includes Daniel Boone's notes and Abraham Lincoln's watch.

★ **Kentucky Vietnam Veterans Memorial:** This memorial takes the form of a large sundial. It honors the 1,103 Kentuckians lost in the Vietnam War. The shadow cast by the sundial points to each veteran's name on the anniversary of his or her death.

Louisville

★ *Belle of Louisville* **steamboat:** For a unique view of Louisville, take a ride down the Ohio River on the *Belle of Louisville*, an old-fashioned 1914 stern-wheeler. The oldest serving steamboat of her type, the *Belle* is a National Historic Landmark.

★ **J. B. Speed Art Museum:** This is Kentucky's oldest and largest art museum, opened in 1927. Visit the Art Sparks Interactive Gallery, where you can create your own masterpiece, design and build a model city, and dance inside a video work of art.

★ **Louisville Science Center:** This is Kentucky's largest hands-on science center. Experience what it's like to drive a bus or fly an airplane, or take a tour of the human body.

★ **Louisville Zoo:** Stroll through Gorilla Forest, tour the Australian Outback, and visit an Indonesian Village, where you can check out tigers and orangutans. And if you're into creepy, crawly creatures, the zoo has one of the world's largest collections of spiders.

Giraffe and visitor at the Louisville Zoo

SEE IT HERE!

SLUGGERS

Louisville Sluggers are the most famous baseball bats in the world. And guess where they're made! You can't miss the Louisville Slugger Museum & Factory. Out front is a bat standing 120 feet (37 m) and weighing 68,000 pounds (31,000 kg). (There's also a giant glove holding a ball, carved out of a 15-ton piece of limestone.) You can take a tour of the factory and order a miniature bat with your own name carved into it.

Louisville Slugger Museum and Factory

★ **Louisville Bats:** The Bats are the top minor-league team of the big-league Cincinnati Reds. See them in action at Louisville Slugger Field.

★ **Kentucky Derby Museum:** The Kentucky Derby has been called "the most exciting two minutes in sports." At this museum, you can catch some of that excitement. Check out the video *The Greatest Race*, and climb atop a model racehorse to feel what it's like to be a jockey.

Hodgenville

★ **Abraham Lincoln Birthplace National Historic Site:** Climb 56 steps (one for each year of Lincoln's life) and you'll reach the impressive granite memorial. Inside you'll find a log cabin that is the 16th president's "symbolic birthplace."

Bardstown

★ **My Old Kentucky Home State Park:** Kentucky's state song is "My Old Kentucky Home." According to legend, Stephen Collins Foster wrote the song after visiting his cousins' home in Bardstown. The house is now part of this state park. It's pictured on Kentucky's state quarter, but you can see it up close here.

SEE IT HERE!

VISIT THE PAST

Kentucky is a great place to go back in time. At Old Fort Harrod State Park in Harrodsburg, you can visit a reproduction of the 1775 fort that was Kentucky's first pioneer settlement and see demonstrations of frontier crafts by workers in costume. Fort Boonesborough State Park has a re-creation of another early Kentucky fort, this one founded by Daniel Boone. Mountain HomePlace in Paintsville is a working farm with a blacksmith shop and schoolhouse. Costumed workers show what farm life was like in Kentucky in the 1850s. At the Shaker Village of Pleasant Hill near Harrodsburg, you can get a glimpse of life in the 1800s in a Shaker settlement. The Shakers were a religious group who lived in communities where they made everything they needed. Shaker crafts and furniture are still highly valued. Visitors to Pleasant Hill can see dance and crafts presentations.

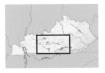

SOUTH CENTRAL KENTUCKY

THINGS TO DO: See where one of America's favorite cars is made, take a scenic ride on an old-time railroad, and go deep belowground in the world's longest cave system.

Stearns

★ **Big South Fork Scenic Railway:** At this must-see for locomotive lovers, take a 16-mile (26 km) round-trip through deep canyons and alongside beautiful streams to Blue Heron, once the site of a thriving mining camp.

Mammoth Cave

★ **Mammoth Cave National Park:** Put on your hard hat and head-lamp and explore the longest cave system in the world. You'll walk, crawl, and squeeze through narrow passages deep belowground and see famous mineral formations such as Frozen Niagara. Back aboveground, you can canoe or kayak on the Green and Nolin rivers.

Horse Cave

★ **Hidden River Cave and American Cave Museum:** Naturalist John Muir called the cave "a noble gateway . . . to the mineral kingdom." You'll want to see what has been called the "world's largest cave entrance." And the museum will give you an in-depth look at the strange and wonderful world of caves.

Bowling Green

★ **Beech Bend Park:** What's a Kentucky Rumbler? It's the hair-raising roller coaster at this amusement and water park. And if you have a need for speed, the park includes an auto-racing oval and drag strip.

★ **Kentucky Museum:** You'll learn what it was like to be a kid in 1800s Kentucky when you check out the old-fashioned toys and musical instruments at this museum on the campus of Western Kentucky University.

★ **Hardin Planetarium:** This space place at Western Kentucky University will have you seeing stars. Sit back and enjoy the star show inside its 40-foot (12 m) dome.

★ **National Corvette Museum:** You can learn about how one of America's favorite sports cars is made and see models from the past 50 years!

National Corvette Museum

Visitors at Dinosaur World

Cave City

★ **Dinosaur World:** This place has about 100 life-sized versions of the beasts. Join in the dino dig—and watch out for *T. rex*!

★ **Kentucky Down Under:** This interactive nature park brings Australian wildlife to the heart of Kentucky. Walk among the wallabies, learn about the music of the didgeridoo (a traditional Australian instrument), and pitch a boomerang—watch out, it's coming back!

Hopkinsville

★ **Trail of Tears Commemorative Park:** This park serves as a memorial to the long journey Cherokees made after they were forced to leave their homes in the Appalachian Mountains.

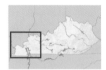

WESTERN KENTUCKY

THINGS TO DO: Climb into a giant bird's nest, get up close and personal with some bison, and create your own river.

Golden Pond

★ **Land Between the Lakes National Recreation Area:** See the area's landscape and wildlife as they existed hundreds of years ago. Hike and canoe at the Woodlands Nature Station. The area is bor-

Land Between the Lakes National Recreation Area

SEE IT HERE!

WICKLIFFE

At Wickliffe Mounds State Historic Site, you can visit a working archaeological site. Archaeologists learn about the past by studying the tools and remains that ancient people have left behind. At Wickliffe Mounds, they have discovered a great deal of information about the first Kentuckians' lives. Some of the pottery and other artifacts excavated here are on display.

dered by Kentucky Lake and Lake Barkley, which were formed by dams made on the Tennessee and Cumberland rivers.

★ **Golden Pond Planetarium:** This place is a real star trip. See the stars and catch a glimpse of solar flares at the observatory. Pick out the constellations on the planetarium's 40-foot (12 m) dome.

Paducah

★ **River Heritage Museum:** Ever wanted to build your own river? This museum lets you move sand and water to configure your own waterway. Fittingly, the museum overlooks the spot where the Tennessee and Ohio rivers meet.

- ★ **Flood wall murals:** The concrete flood wall along Paducah's river-front was built to keep floodwaters out of the city's streets. The scenes painted on the wall depict moments from the city's history, from its founding to the steamboat era of the late 1800s and beyond.
- ★ **Horse-drawn carriage rides:** Take in historic and scenic downtown Paducah in style. Among the many sights, you'll see the brick sidewalks of Broadway and century-old buildings.
- ★ **Museum of the American Quilter's Society:** Paducah is called Quilt City, U.S.A., and this museum is one of the reasons why. It's the largest museum in the world devoted to quilts. You can see more than 150 examples of this beloved art form.

Henderson

- ★ **John James Audubon State Park:** This place is for the birds—and kids will love it. Named for the 19th-century artist famous for his paintings of birds, this park is in prime bird-watching country. Be sure to visit the Discovery Center for an interactive introduction to the world of birds, complete with a giant bird's nest.

Owensboro

- ★ **International Bluegrass Museum:** Bluegrass is an essential part of Kentucky's culture, and this is the place to learn about the great musicians who made its history. Listen in on a jam session, make your selection from a bluegrass jukebox, and learn about Bill Monroe, the Father of Bluegrass.

Fort Knox

- ★ **U.S. Bullion Depository:** Sorry, no visitors allowed inside the steel and concrete vaults that protect the U.S. gold supplies. Still, visitors like to stop outside the gates to take photographs of the historic gold vaults.
- ★ **General George Patton Museum:** This museum traces the history of armored vehicles and tells how they have changed the way wars are fought. Named for World War II general George S. Patton, it also includes a section of the Berlin Wall that divided East and West Berlin during the cold war.

Bass fiddle at the International Bluegrass Museum

SCIENCE, TECHNOLOGY, & MATH PROJECTS

Make weather maps, graph population statistics, and research endangered species that live in the state.

120

PRIMARY VS. SECONDARY SOURCES

121

So what are primary and secondary sources? And what's the diff? This section explains all that and where you can find them.

BIOGRAPHICAL DICTIONARY

133

This at-a-glance guide highlights some of the state's most important and influential people. Visit this section and read about their contributions to the state, the country, and the world.

RESOURCES

Books, Web sites, DVDs, and more. Take a look at these additional sources for information about the state.

137

WRITING PROJECTS

★ ★ ★

Write a Memoir, Journal, or Editorial for Your School Newspaper!

Picture Yourself . . .

★ Living on the frontier. Imagine what life was like for Daniel Boone and others during that time. What kind of house would you have? And what kind of food would you eat? How would you spend your days?

   SEE: Chapter Three, page 43.

★ At the Kentucky Derby. Maybe you are a trainer or a jockey for a promising horse. Or maybe you just came to watch an exciting race. Describe the sights and sounds of Churchill Downs.

   SEE: Chapter Six, page 83.

Create an Election Brochure or Web Site!

Run for office!

Throughout this book, you've read about some of the issues that concern Kentucky today. As a candidate for governor of Kentucky, create a campaign brochure or Web site. Explain how you meet the qualifications to be governor of Kentucky, and talk about the three or four major issues you'll focus on if you are elected. Remember, you'll be responsible for Kentucky's budget. How would you spend the taxpayers' money?

SEE: Chapter Seven, pages 84–93.

GO TO: Kentucky's government Web site at www.kentucky.gov/

Compare and Contrast —When, Why, and How Did They Come?

Compare the migrations and explorations of the first Native people and the first European explorers. Tell about:

★ When their migrations began

★ How they traveled

★ Why they migrated

★ Where their journeys began and ended

★ What they found when they arrived

   SEE: Chapters Two and Three, pages 22–43.

Settlers crossing into Kentucky through the Cumberland Gap

ART PROJECTS

★ ★ ★

Create a PowerPoint Presentation or Visitors' Guide

Welcome to Kentucky!

Kentucky is a great place to visit and to live! From its natural beauty to its bustling cities and historic sites, there's plenty to see and do. In your PowerPoint presentation or brochure, highlight 10 to 15 of Kentucky's stunning landmarks. Be sure to include:

★ a map of the state showing where these sites are located

★ photos, illustrations, Web links, natural history facts, geographic stats, climate and weather info, and descriptions of plants and wildlife.

SEE: Chapter Nine, pages 104–115.

GO TO: The official Web site of Kentucky's tourism at www.kentuckytourism.com. Download and print maps, photos, national landmark images, and vacation ideas for tourists.

Illustrate the Lyrics to the Kentucky State Song

("My Old Kentucky Home")

Use markers, paints, photos, collages, colored pencils, or computer graphics to illustrate the lyrics to "My Old Kentucky Home," the state song. Turn your illustrations into a picture book, or scan them into PowerPoint and add music.

SEE: The lyrics to "My Old Kentucky Home" on page 128.

GO TO: The Kentucky state Web site at www.kentucky.gov/ to find out more about the origin of the Kentucky state song.

Research Kentucky's State Quarter

From 1999 to 2008, the U.S. Mint introduced new quarters commemorating each of the 50 states in the order that they were admitted into the Union. Each state's quarter features a unique design on its reverse, or back.

GO TO: www.usmint.gov/kids and find out what's featured on the back of the Kentucky quarter.

Research and write an essay explaining:

★ the significance of each image

★ who designed the quarter

★ who chose the final design

Design your own Kentucky state quarter. What images would you choose for the reverse?

★ Make a poster showing the Kentucky quarter and label each image.

SCIENCE, TECHNOLOGY, & MATH PROJECTS

★   ★   ★

Graph Population Statistics!

★ Compare population statistics (such as ethnic background, birth, death, and literacy rates) in Kentucky counties or major cities.

★ In your graph or chart, look at population density. Write sentences describing what the population statistics show. Graph one set of population statistics, and write a paragraph explaining what the graphs reveal.

SEE: Chapter Six, pages 71–72.

GO TO: The official Web site for the U.S. Census Bureau at www.census.gov, and at http://quickfacts.census.gov/qfd/states/21000.html, to find out more about population statistics, how they work, and what the statistics are for Kentucky.

Kentucky student

Create a Weather Map of Kentucky!

Use your knowledge of Kentucky's geography to research and identify conditions that result in specific weather events. What is it about the geography of Kentucky that makes it vulnerable to things such as earthquakes? Create a weather map or poster that shows the weather patterns over the state. To accompany your map, explain the technology used to measure weather phenomena.

SEE: Chapter One, pages 16–17.

GO TO: The National Oceanic and Atmospheric Administration's National Weather Service Web site at www.weather.gov for weather maps and forecasts for Kentucky.

Track Endangered Species

★ Using your knowledge of Kentucky's wildlife, research which animals and plants are endangered or threatened. Find out what the state is doing to protect these species.

★ Chart known populations of the animals and plants, and report on changes in certain geographical areas

SEE: Chapter One, page 21.

GO TO: Sites such as www.endangeredspecie.com/states/ky.htm

PRIMARY VS. SECONDARY SOURCES

★ ★ ★

What's the Diff?

Your teacher may require at least one or two primary sources and one or two secondary sources for your assignment. So, what's the difference between the two?

★ **Primary sources are original.** You are reading the actual words of someone's diary, journal, letter, autobiography, or interview. Primary sources can also be photographs, maps, prints, cartoons, news/film footage, posters, first-person newspaper articles, drawings, musical scores, and recordings. By the way, when you conduct a survey, interview someone, shoot a video, or take photographs to include in a project, you are creating primary sources!

★ **Secondary sources are what you find in encyclopedias, textbooks, articles, biographies, and almanacs.** These are written by a person or group of people who tell about something that happened to someone else. Secondary sources also recount what another person said or did. This book is an example of a secondary source.

Now that you know what primary sources are—where can you find them?

★ **Your school or local library:** Check the library catalog for collections of original writings, government documents, musical scores, and so on. Some of this material may be stored on microfilm. The Library of Congress Web site (www.loc.gov) is an excellent online resource for primary source materials.

★ **Historical societies:** These organizations keep historical documents, photographs, and other materials. Staff members can help you find what you are looking for. History museums are also great places to see primary sources firsthand.

★ **The Internet:** There are lots of sites that have primary sources you can download and use in a project or assignment.

TIMELINE

★ ★ ★

U.S. Events 1400 **Kentucky Events**

1492

Christopher Columbus and his crew sight land in the Caribbean Sea.

1400–1700

Shawnee, Cherokee, and Chickasaw groups thrive in the region.

1600

1607

The first permanent English settlement in North America is established at Jamestown.

Jacques Marquette

1620

Pilgrims found Plymouth Colony, the second permanent English settlement.

1673

Jacques Marquette explores the Mississippi River.

1682

René-Robert Cavelier, Sieur de La Salle, claims more than 1 million square miles (2.6 million sq km) of territory in the Mississippi River basin for France, naming it Louisiana.

1700

1750s

Shawnees live in a village called Eskippakithiki in Kentucky.

1750

Thomas Walker crosses into Kentucky through the Cumberland Gap.

1755–63

England and France fight over North American colonial lands in the French and Indian War. By the end of the war, France has ceded all of its land west of the Mississippi to Spain and its Canadian territories to England.

1774

James Harrod leads settlers into Kentucky.

1775

Daniel Boone cuts the Wilderness Road from Cumberland Gap into Kentucky.

1776

Thirteen American colonies declare their independence from Great Britain.

1776

The Virginia legislature creates Kentucky County.

U.S. Events

1787
The U.S. Constitution is written.

1803
The Louisiana Purchase almost doubles the size of the United States.

1812–15
The United States and Great Britain fight the War of 1812.

1830
The Indian Removal Act forces eastern Native American groups to relocate west of the Mississippi River.

1861–65
The American Civil War is fought between the Northern Union and the Southern Confederacy; it ends with the surrender of the Confederate army, led by General Robert E. Lee.

1863
President Abraham Lincoln frees all slaves in the Southern Confederacy with the Emancipation Proclamation.

1917–18
The United States engages in World War I.

Kentucky Events

1778
The Shawnee attack Boonesborough.

1792
Kentucky becomes the 15th state; the constitutional convention permits slavery in Kentucky.

1800

1812–15
More than 25,000 Kentuckians fight in the War of 1812.

1818
The Chickasaw are forced to give up their land in Kentucky.

1838
U.S. government orders Cherokees to leave their homeland in the Appalachian Mountains.

1862
Civil War battles are fought at Richmond and Perryville.

1870–1900
Industry expands in Kentucky.

1875
The first Kentucky Derby is run in Louisville.

1900

1904
The Black Patch War breaks out in western Kentucky.

U.S. Events

1929
The stock market crashes, plunging the United States more deeply into the Great Depression.

1941–45
The United States engages in World War II.

1951–53
The United States engages in the Korean War.

1954
The U.S. Supreme Court prohibits segregation of public schools in the *Brown v. Board of Education* ruling.

1964–73
The United States engages in the Vietnam War.

1991
The United States and other nations engage in the brief Persian Gulf War against Iraq.

2001
Terrorists hijack four U.S. aircraft and crash them into the World Trade Center in New York City, the Pentagon in Arlington, Virginia, and a Pennsylvania field, killing thousands.

2003
The United States and coalition forces invade Iraq.

Kentucky Events

1930
Drought strikes Kentucky.

1945
The Kentucky Dam is completed.

Kentucky Dam

1966
The Kentucky legislature passes a strong civil rights law.

1990
The Kentucky legislature passes a law to reform the education system.

2000

Toyota plant in Georgetown

2006
Toyota begins making hybrid Camrys in Georgetown.

GLOSSARY

★ ★ ★

bluff a high, steep bank

chert a rock resembling flint

constitutional relating to a written document that states the main principles around which a political body will be organized to guide its government

distilleries places where alcoholic products such as whiskey are produced

economy the system of producing and consuming goods and services in a community

eroded slowly eaten away at and destroyed

escarpments long, steep cliffs

isolated set apart from others

labor unions organizations of workers formed to protect the rights of their members, including, especially, better pay and working conditions

livestock farm animals such as cows and hogs

longhouses long buildings made and used by Native American communities

militia an army made up of citizens trained to serve as soldiers in an emergency

moats deep, wide trenches filled with water that surround and protect forts or other places

municipalities self-governing cities or towns

palisades fences of logs set vertically into the ground close to each other to create protected villages

pelts animal skins covered in fur

renovated cleaned, improved, or rebuilt

sandstone a type of rock made of sand cemented together by another material

segregation separation from others, according to race, class, ethnic group, religion, or other factors

seismologists scientists who study earthquakes

sit-ins acts of protest that involve sitting in racially segregated places and refusing to leave

sloughs wet and marshy places, such as swamps

stockades enclosures of posts designed to protect against attack

tributaries smaller rivers that flow into a larger river

FAST FACTS

★　★　★

State Symbols

State seal

Statehood date	June 1, 1792, the 15th state
Origin of state name	Perhaps from the Iroquoian word often translated as "place of meadows"
State capital	Frankfort
State nickname	Bluegrass State
State motto	"United We Stand, Divided We Fall"
State bird	Cardinal
State flower	Goldenrod
State fish	Kentucky Spotted Bass
State gemstone	Freshwater pearl
State mineral	Coal
State song	"My Old Kentucky Home"
State tree	Tulip poplar
State wild animal	Gray squirrel
State fossil	Brachiopod
State butterfly	Viceroy butterfly
State horse	Thoroughbred
State fair	Louisville (mid-August)

Geography

Tulip poplar blossom

Total area; rank	40,409 square miles (104,659 sq km); 37th
Land; rank	39,728 square miles (102,896 sq km); 36th
Water; rank	681 square miles (1,764 sq km); 38th
Inland water; rank	681 square miles (1,764 sq km); 31st
Geographic center	Marion, 3 miles (5 km) north-northwest of Lebanon
Latitude	36° 30′ N to 39° 9′ N
Longitude	81° 58′ W to 89° 34′ W
Highest point	Black Mountain at 4,145 feet (1,263 m)
Lowest point	At the Mississippi River, 257 feet (78 m)
Largest city	Louisville
Number of counties	120
Longest river	Ohio River

Population

Population; rank (2006 estimate)	4,206,074; 26th
Density (2006 estimate)	106 persons per square mile (41 per sq km)
Population distribution (2000 census)	55% urban, 45% rural
Ethnic distribution (2005 estimate)	White persons: 90.4%*
	Black persons: 7.5%*
	Asian persons: 0.9%*
	American Indian and Alaska Native persons: 0.2%*
	Native Hawaiian and Other Pacific Islander: 0.0%*
	Persons reporting two or more races: 1.0%
	Persons of Hispanic or Latino origin: 2.0%†
	White persons not Hispanic: 88.6%

* Hispanics may be of any race, so they are also included in applicable race categories.
† Includes persons reporting only one race.

Weather

Record high temperature	114°F (46°C) at Greensburg on July 28, 1930
Record low temperature	−37°F (−38°C) at Shelbyville on January 19, 1994
Average July temperature	78°F (26°C)
Average January temperature	33°F (1°C)
Average annual precipitation	45 inches (114 cm)

State flag

STATE SONG

★ ★ ★

"My Old Kentucky Home"

Written by Stephen Foster, the song became popular in the early 1850s. It was chosen as the state song in 1928. "My Old Kentucky Home" is played before the Kentucky Derby race, and it is played by just about every high school band in the state.

The sun shines bright in the old Kentucky home,
'Tis summer, the people are gay,
the corn top's ripe and the meadow's in the
    bloom,
While the birds make music all the day.
The young folks roll on the little cabin floor,
All merry, all happy, and bright.
By'n by hard times comes a-knocking at the door,
Then my old Kentucky home, good night.

Chorus:
Weep no more, my lady,
Oh! Weep no more today
We will sing one song for the old Kentucky home,
For the old Kentucky home far away.

They hunt no more for the 'possum and the coon,
On meadow, the hill and the shore.
They sing no more by the glimmer of the moon,
On the bench by that old cabin door.
The day goes by like a shadow o'er the heart,
With sorrow where all was delight.
The time has come when the people have to part,
Then my old Kentucky home, good night.

The head must bow and the back will have to
    bend,
Wherever the people may go;
A few more days and the trouble all will end
In the field where sugar-canes may grow.
A few more days for to tote the weary load,
No matter, 'twill never be light.
A few more days till we totter on the road,
then my old Kentucky home, good night.

NATURAL AREAS AND HISTORIC SITES

National Park
Kentucky's sole national park, *Mammoth Cave National Park*, is the longest recorded cave system in the world.

National Recreation Area
Kentucky's Big South Fork National River & Recreation Area encompasses 125,000 acres (50,585 ha) of the Cumberland Plateau, and protects the free-flowing Big South Fork of the Cumberland River and its tributaries.

National Historic Trail
Trail of Tears National Historic Trail weaves its way through Kentucky as part of the pathway that was used by Cherokees as they were forced to move westward through nine states.

National Historical Park
Kentucky's lone national historical park, the *Cumberland Gap National Historical Park*, commemorates the mountain pass in the Appalachian Mountains that was an important route for westward settlers.

National Historic Site
Kentucky takes great pride in its only national historic site, the *Abraham Lincoln Birthplace National Historic Site*, which contains a replica of the cabin where the 16th president of the United States was born.

National Forest
Kentucky's sole national forest, the *Daniel Boone National Forest*, is located along the Cumberland Plateau in the Appalachian foothills of eastern Kentucky. The forest encompasses more than 707,000 acres (286,110 ha) of mostly rugged terrain, characterized by steep forested ridges, narrow ravines, and more than 3,400 miles (5,472 km) of sandstone cliffs.

State Parks and Forests
Kentucky supports a system of 52 beautiful state parks and recreation areas, including *Wickliffe Mounds State Historic Site, Jefferson Davis State Historic Site, Cumberland Falls State Resort Park,* and *Dr. Thomas Walker State Historic Site.*

SPORTS TEAMS

★ ★ ★

NCAA Teams (Division I)

Eastern Kentucky University *Colonels*
Morehead State University *Eagles*
Murray State University *Racers*
University of Kentucky *Wildcats*
University of Louisville *Cardinals*
Western Kentucky University *Hilltoppers*

A basketball game at the University of Kentucky

C**U**LTU**R**AL INSTIT**U**TI**O**NS

★ ★ ★

Libraries

Filson Club Historical Society (Louisville) has a fine collection on Kentucky history.

Kentucky Historical Society (Frankfort) contains a large Kentuckian collection.

Louisville Free Public Library is the largest public library system in the state.

State Law Library (Frankfort) houses a rare collection of law books and resources.

Museums

Bluegrass Scenic Railroad & Museum (Versailles) preserves and displays artifacts of Central Kentucky's railroad history.

Coca-Cola Memorabilia (Elizabethtown) displays antique Coca-Cola delivery vehicles, turn-of-the-20th-century bottling works, vending machines, toys, bottle displays, signs, an expanded Santa exhibit, and the only complete collection of classic Coca-Cola serving trays known to exist.

Explorium of Lexington (Lexington) features nine discovery zones with interactive exhibits.

Fort Knox is the home of the nation's gold depository and the *General George Patton Museum*. Visitors are not permitted inside the depository.

Kentucky Military History Museum (Frankfort) emphasizes the service of the Kentucky Militia, State Guard, and other volunteer military organizations, from the Revolution through the Gulf War.

The Old State Capitol (Frankfort) is home to the *Kentucky Historical Society* and houses the *State Law Library*.

Shaker Village of Pleasant Hill (Harrodsburg) features a restoration of the 19th-century Shaker community.

Performing Arts

Kentucky has one major opera company, one major symphony orchestra, one major dance company, and one major professional theater company.

Universities and Colleges

In 2006, Kentucky had 26 public and 44 private institutions of higher learning.

ANNUAL EVENTS

January–March

Land Between the Lakes Eagles Weekend (February)

Humana Festival of New American Plays in Louisville (March–April)

April–June

Keeneland Race Track Spring Meet in Lexington (April)

Rolex Kentucky 3-day Event in Lexington (April)

Dogwood Trail Celebration in Paducah (April)

Kentucky Derby Festival in Louisville (April–May)

Kentucky Guild of Artists and Craftsmen's Spring Fair in Berea (May)

International Bar-B-Q Festival in Owensboro (May)

Glasgow Highland Games in Glasgow (June)

Shaker Festival in South Union (late June)

July–September

Kentucky State Fair in Louisville (August)

IBMA Bluegrass Fan Fest in Owensboro (September)

Corn Island Storytelling Festival in Louisville (September)

World Chicken Festival in London (September)

October–December

Kentucky Guild of Artists and Craftsmen's Fall Fair in Berea (October)

Daniel Boone Festival in Barbourville (October)

Allen County Singing Festival (October)

Perryville Battlefield Commemoration (October)

Equifestival of Kentucky in Lexington (October)

North American International Livestock Expo in Louisville (November)

Southern Lights at the Kentucky Horse Park in Lexington (November–December)

Christmas Sing in the cave at Mammoth Cave National Park (December)

BIOGRAPHICAL DICTIONARY

Muhammad Ali See page 82.

John James Audubon (1785–1851) was a naturalist and wildlife illustrator. He lived in Kentucky from 1808 to 1821 and roamed the state observing and drawing birds. His *Birds of America* is a collection of 435 life-sized prints of birds. The National Audubon Society was named in his honor.

Alben W. Barkley (1877–1956) represented Kentucky in both branches of Congress and was vice president of the United States from 1949 to 1953.

Daniel Carter Beard (1850–1941) founded the Boy Scouts of America in 1910.

James G. Birney See page 51.

Stephen Bishop See page 14.

Blackfish See page 39.

Daniel Boone See page 38.

William Wells Brown

George Rogers Clark

Madeline Breckinridge (1872–1920), the great-granddaughter of Senator Henry Clay, crusaded for the voting rights of Kentucky women.

Mary Breckinridge See page 62.

William Wells Brown (1814?–1884) was born into slavery in Lexington and became one of the most dynamic abolitionist speakers and writers. He is considered the first African American novelist and playwright.

Kit Carson (1809–1868) was born in Madison County. He was a frontiersman, guide, and cavlaryman, who led campaigns to remove Native Americans from their lands.

Albert Benjamin "Happy" Chandler See page 91.

George Rogers Clark (1752–1818) was an American military leader on the western frontier in the American Revolution. He later helped found Louisville.

134

Lewis Clarke (1812–1897), born into slavery in Madison County, escaped to freedom and became a nationally known antislavery speaker. After his death, his body lay in state at the City Auditorium in Lexington, the first time an African American was accorded this honor in Kentucky.

Cassius M. Clay (1810–1903) was a lawyer, politician, and newspaper publisher known for his strong antislavery stance.

Henry Clay (1777–1852) served as a Kentucky senator and representative, and as U.S. secretary of state. He lost three times in races for the presidency. He once said, "I'd rather be right than president."

Laura Clay See page 59.

George Clooney (1961–) is an actor and movie director. He was born in Lexington.

Rosemary Clooney (1928–2002) was one of America's top jazz and pop singers in the 1950s and 1960s. She was born in Maysville.

George Clooney

Crystal Gayle

John Colgan (1840–?) was a Louisville pharmacist who invented the first flavored chewing gum in 1879. He called it Taffy Tolu.

Martha Layne Collins See page 89.

Tom Cruise (1962–) is an actor who starred in *Mission Impossible* and many other movies. He was raised in Louisville.

Jefferson Davis (1808–1889) was president of the Confederacy during the Civil War. He was born in Christian County (now Todd County).

Johnny Depp See page 81.

John Filson See page 15.

Ernie Fletcher (1952–) Born in Mt. Sterling, Fletcher was elected governor in 2003.

Crystal Gayle (1951–) was born in Paintsville and became a country music performer.

Josiah Henson (1789–1883) was an escaped Kentucky slave who helped publish the antislavery newspaper *Voice of the Fugitive*. He may have been the model for Uncle Tom, the leading character in Harriet Beecher Stowe's novel *Uncle Tom's Cabin*.

Mary Draper Ingles (1732–1815) was probably the first white woman to visit Kentucky. She was living in Virginia when she and her sons were captured by a Shawnee war party in 1755. She traveled to Kentucky with the Shawnee, but after three months, escaped. It took her 40 days to walk back to her home in Virginia.

Casey Jones (1864–1900) was a train engineer whose skill was celebrated in popular songs. He lived in Kentucky for many years.

Ashley Judd (1968–) is an actor who starred in *Divine Secrets of the Ya-Ya Sisterhood* and other movies. She was born in California but grew up in Kentucky.

Naomi Judd (1946–), with her daughter Wynonna, formed the country music singing duo The Judds. Also the mother of actor Ashley Judd, she was born in Ashland.

Ashley Judd

Wynonna Judd (1964–) formed the country music duo The Judds with her mother, Naomi, then went on to have a successful solo career. She was born in Ashland.

Abraham Lincoln See page 92.

Mary Todd Lincoln (1818–1882) was born in Lexington and married Abraham Lincoln in 1842. She became first lady when he won the presidency in 1861.

Loretta Lynn See page 79.

Bobbie Ann Mason (1940–) is a writer of acclaimed novels and short stories set in the South. She was born in Mayfield.

Natachee Scott Momaday (1913–) is a Fairview-born poet and teacher of Cherokee, French, and English descent. In 1972, she edited a classroom reader, *American Indian Authors*, the first collection of stories by Native American authors for children. She is the mother of acclaimed writer N. Scott Momaday.

Bill Monroe See page 78.

Bobbie Ann Mason

Thomas Hunt Morgan (1866–1945) earned a Nobel Prize in 1933 for his scientific research into the ways characteristics are passed from parents to offspring. He was born in Lexington.

Carrie Nation (1846–1911) was born in Garrard County. She was a member of the Women's Christian Temperance Union, and was known for wielding a hatchet to smash saloons and establishments that served alcohol.

Suzy Post See page 63.

Pee Wee Reese (1918–1999) was elected to the Baseball Hall of Fame for his skill as an infielder for the Brooklyn and Los Angeles Dodgers. He was born and raised in Louisville.

Harland Sanders See page 103.

Diane Sawyer (1945–) is a television reporter who launched her career at a Louisville TV station.

Mary Levi Smith

Isaac Shelby (1750–1826) led American troops in the American Revolution and the War of 1812. He was Kentucky's first governor, serving from 1792 to 1796 and again from 1812 to 1816.

Ricky Skaggs (1954–), born in Cordell, is a Grammy and Country Music Association award-winning musician, composer, and writer, praised for his skill as a mandolin player.

Mary Levi Smith See page 74.

Zachary Taylor See page 92.

Thomas Walker (1715–1794), a physician and surveyor, led the first pioneer expedition into Kentucky in 1750.

Whitepath See page 48.

Dwight Yoakam (1956–) was born in Pikeville and is an actor and country music performer.

Whitney M. Young Jr. See page 64.

Diane Sawyer

RESOURCES

BOOKS

Nonfiction

Anderson, Peter. *John James Audubon*. New York: Franklin Watts, 2005.

Buckley, James Jr. *Muhammad Ali*. Milwaukee, Wis.: World Almanac Library, 2004.

Burgan, Michael. *Henry Clay: The Great Compromiser*. Chanhassen, Minn.: Child's World, 2004.

Freedman, Russell. *Lincoln: A Photobiography*. New York: Clarion, 1987.

Furbee, Mary R. *Shawnee Captive: The Story of Mary Draper Ingles*. Greensboro, N.C.: Morgan Reynolds, 2001.

Graff, Mike. *Mammoth Cave National Park*. Mankato, Minn.: Bridgestone, 2004.

Kent, Deborah. *The Trail of Tears*. New York: Children's Press, 2005.

Santella, Andrew. *Daniel Boone and the Cumberland Gap*. New York: Children's Press, 2002.

Fiction

Creech, Sharon. *Chasing Redbird*. Waterville, Maine: Thorndike Press, 2005.

Crum, Shutta. *Spitting Image*. New York: Clarion Books, 2003.

Davis, Jenny. *Good-bye and Keep Cold*. New York: Orchard Books, 1987.

Forman, James D. *A Ballad for Hogskin Hill*. New York: Farrar Straus & Giroux, 1979.

Lyon, George Ella. *Borrowed Children*. Lexington, KY: University Press of Kentucky, 1999.

Rinaldi, Ann. *The Coffin Quilt: The Feud between the Hatfields and the McCoys*. New York: Gulliver Books, 2001.

WEB SITES AND ORGANIZATIONS

The Commonwealth of Kentucky

www.kentucky.gov/
This is Kentucky's official Web site, where you can learn about the state government and its political leaders.

Discovering Northern Kentucky's Past

www.nku.edu/~anthro/nkuanthromuseum/FAweb/index.htm
From Northern Kentucky University, this site is filled with information about how archaeologists learn about ancient Native American cultures.

Kentucky AWAKE Plants and Wildlife

www.kentuckyawake.org/plantsWildlife/
Visit this site to get an introduction to the plants and animals of Kentucky.

Kentucky Coal Education

www.coaleducation.org/
Learn about Kentucky's coal mining heritage.

Kentucky Department for Libraries and Archives

www.kdla.ky.gov/resources.htm
This site has everything from Kentucky's most popular baby names to a history of Kentucky's capitals.

Kentucky Department of Tourism

www.kentuckytourism.com/
Go to this site to learn more about great places to visit.

Kentucky Historical Society

http://history.ky.gov/
You can find more details about the history of Kentucky at this site.

Kentucky Kids Pages

http://kentucky.gov/Portal/Category/fac_kids
Check out these links for kids, from the Commonwealth of Kentucky's official site.

Kentucky State Parks

www.parks.ky.gov
You can find information about Kentucky's state parks and historic sites.

Kentucky's Flora and Fauna

www.biology.eku.edu/KOS/kyflorafauna.html
This Eastern Kentucky University site provides information on Kentucky's plants and animals.

Kentucky's Underground Railroad

www.ket.org/underground/
Learn how the Underground Railroad helped enslaved people find freedom.

INDEX

★ ★ ★

AUTHOR'S TIPS AND SOURCE NOTES

★ ★ ★

It's no surprise that one of Kentucky's early settlers, John Filson, wrote a book about his new home. Since Filson published his *The Discovery, Settlement and Present State of Kentucke* in 1784, there have always been resources for readers who want to know more about the Bluegrass State. I consulted some of the best works to help me prepare this book.

A New History of Kentucky by Lowell H. Harrison and James C. Klotter (1997) provided a comprehensive overview of Kentucky's past. *Atlas of Kentucky* (Richard Ulack, editor-in-chief) offered a wealth of information on the environment, economy and people of Kentucky. Its many maps, graphs, and illustrations made it a beautiful book to use, too. John Mack Faragher's *Daniel Boone* reintroduced me to Kentucky's most famous early settler and supplied insights into life on the Kentucky frontier.

I also consulted many of the online resources offered by Kentucky's universities and its state agencies. For example, Northern Kentucky University's Web site "Discovering Northern Kentucky's Past" (www.nku.edu/~anthro/nkuanthromuseum/FAweb/) is filled with information about Kentucky's prehistoric Native people. And the Kentucky Department for Libraries and Archives site (www.kdla.ky.gov/resources.htm) has fun facts about everything from Kentucky's capitol buildings to how its counties got their names.